INDIAN POLITICS SINCE THE MUTINY

INDIAN POLITICS SINCE THE MUTINY:

BEING AN ACCOUNT OF THE DEVELOPMENT OF PUBLIC LIFE AND POLITICAL INSTITUTIONS AND OF PROMINENT POLITICAL PERSONALITIES

CHINTAMANI C.YAJNESWARA

GYAN

Published by

Gyan Publishing House
5, Ansari Road
Daryaganj, New Delhi-110002
Phone: 011-47034999, 9811692060
E-mail: books@gyanbooks.com

Distribution Network
gyanbooks.com
India, USA, Canada, UK, Australia

ISBN: 978-93-7014-199-5 (HB)

First Published, 1937

2nd Impression 2025

Printed at: Gyan Press, Delhi.

INDIAN POLITICS SINCE THE MUTINY
Author: CHINTAMANI C.YAJNESWARA

Indian Politics since the Mutiny

Being an Account of the Development of Public Life and Political Institutions and of Prominent Political Personalities

BY

C. Y. CHINTAMANI

Chief Editor, the 'Leader', Allahabad

(*Lectures delivered at the Andhra University on Nov.* 28, 29 & 30 *and Dec.* 1, 1935 *under the terms of the Sir Alladi Krishnaswami Endowment*)

WALTAIR

Printed by Krishna Ram Mehta at the Leader Press, Allahabad, and published by the Registrar, Andhra University, Waltair

1937

SRI GOPAL KRISHNA GOKHALE
May 1866—February 1915

To

THE ADORED MEMORY OF

My Political Guru

SRI GOPAL KRISHNA GOKHALE

India's Greatest Patriot-Statesman

in humble gratitude and with profound reverence

PREFACE

INVITED by Sir S. Radhakrishnan, the learned and distinguished Vice-Chancellor of Andhra University[1], to deliver a course of three lectures on a subject of my choice, I accepted the kind invitation and selected the subject "Indian Politics since the Mutiny" on the advice of my friends, the right hon. Sir Tej Bahadur Sapru and Mehta Krishna Ram, the latter my colleague in the conduct of the LEADER[2]. These lectures are called Allady Krishnaswami Iyer Lectures as they were founded, at Sir Radhakrishnan's suggestion, by Sir Allady Krishnaswami Iyer, the learned Advocate-General of Madras. I feel grateful to Sir Radhakrishnan for the honour he did me.

It gave me special pleasure to receive and to accept the invitation as the lectures were to be delivered at the Andhra University and in my native district of Vizagapatam[3]. I ceased to be a resident of the district more than thirty-six years ago but have retained my contacts with relations and friends. In fact, several members of my family still live there. I therefore felt happy at the invitation from a place naturally dear to me.

I owe it to the large audiences, running into thousands, before whom these lectures were delivered, to acknowledge the enormous patience and the charming

---

1. Sir Radhakrishnan has since relinquished the office on appointment to a chair of Ethics and Religion in Oxford University.

2. I desire to express my sense of gratitude to this loving friend who willingly takes over my work in addition to his, to enable me to take part in public activities.

3. I was born at Vizianagram in that district and educated in the Maharaja's College there, thanks to the generous help given by Maharaja Sir Ananda Gajapati Raj, G. C. I. E. My journalistic and public life began at Vizagapatam in 1898.

courtesy that they showed. Intended to be three, the lectures had to be extended to a fourth day owing to their length. I taxed the patience of the hearers for over seven hours, but from beginning to end their attitude was most encouraging. I thank them for their kindness to a brother who, though his lot has long been cast in another part of the country, remains one of them.

I am indebted to my old teacher and constant friend, Mr. M. Venkanna Pantulu, for the labour of love he undertook in preparing the Index. This is the second time he has so obliged me, but he is now thirty-two years older and is over sixty-five. I may be permitted to reproduce what I wrote of him in 1905 :

> My talented friend, Mr. M. Venkanna Pantulu, of the Maharaja's College, Vizianagram, has earned my thanks by laboriously setting himself to prepare the very useful analytical Index which is appended at the end of the work. Perhaps it will not be amiss to say here of my friend, that he is an unusually well-read man—a literary recluse I call him—who because of his habit of 'keeping himself to himself', is not known to the public as he deserves to be.[1]

It is wholly my fault that there has been enormous delay in the publication of these lectures. I apologize therefor to the authorities of Andhra University. Very busy months followed the delivery of the lectures and, thanks to excessive work, declining health and advancing years, I am sorry I was not able to attend earlier to the preparation of the papers for the press.

The text of the lectures is here given to the public as delivered. Where any new matter is inserted it is indicated in foot-notes. A few words interspersed here and there due to happenings after the lectures were delivered, are also relegated to foot-notes.

1. Preface to "Speeches and Writings of Sir Pherozeshah Mehta", edited by C. Y. Chintamani. The Indian Press, Allahabad, 1905.

The subject-matter of the lectures—"Indian Politics since the Mutiny"—is the development of public life and political ideas and institutions in this country during the last seventy-seven years (1858—1935), say three-quarters of a century. The period under review is divided into four parts :

I. The twenty-seven years, say the quarter of a century, that preceded the establishment of the Indian National Congress ;

II. The first twenty years of the Congress (1885-1905);

III. The anti-partition agitation to the non-cooperation movement (1905-1919) ;

IV. The last sixteen years (1919-1935).

"I shall hope" I said, " to illustrate my remarks on the subject by reference to the personalities who may be said to have dominated, or played a leading part in the activities of their day."

The lectures are here divided into chapters and sections for the greater convenience of the readers.

I made every endeavour to avoid unfairness to persons whose opinions I do not share. But I cannot hope to have achieved complete success in the effort, honest as it was. To those—friends or strangers—to whom I may have been unintentionally guilty of any unfairness, I hereby express my regret.

I thank my friend Babu Vishwanath Prasad, general manager of the *Leader* and the *Bharat*, for his kind and able supervision of the printing of this volume.

Allahabad, Nov. 12, 1937 C. Y. CHINTAMANI

TABLE OF CONTENTS

CHAPTER I

THE PERIOD BEFORE THE CONGRESS

CHAPTER II

(1885-1905)

THE CONGRESS (First twenty years)

CHAPTER III

(1905-1919)

PARTITION OF BENGAL AND AFTER

CHAPTER IV

(1919-1935)

NON-COOPERATION AND AFTER

PAGES

PAGES

CHAPTER V

CHAPTER I[1]

I

THE PERIOD BEFORE THE CONGRESS

Public life, as we know it today, may be said to have been non-existent at the beginning of the period of review. The Sepoy Mutiny of 1857 threw everything into confusion and its suppression was followed by the abolition of the East India Company and the assumption of the government of the country direct by the Sovereign. The old Board of Control with its President was replaced by the Secretary of State for India in Council. Queen Victoria signalized her assumption of direct rule by the historic Proclamation which has long been referred to as India's Magna Charta. The following three paragraphs from that memorable state paper may be quoted as justifying the popular title given to the Proclamation :—

The Royal Proclamation of 1858

"We hold ourselves bound to the natives of our Indian territories by the same obligations of duty which bind us to all our other subjects ; and those obligations, by the blessing of Almighty God, we shall faithfully and conscientiously fulfil."

"And it is our further will that, so far as may be, our subjects, of whatever race or creed, be freely and impartially admitted to offices in our service, the duties of which they may be qualified, by their education, ability and integrity. duly to discharge."

"It is our earnest desire to stimulate the peaceful industry of India, to promote works of public utility and improvement, and to administer its government for the benefit of all our subjects resident therein. In their prosperity will be our strength; in their contentment our security and in their

1. The chapters correspond to the Lectures with minor variations. Due to exigencies of time and the unequal length of the chapters, two formed one lecture and again, one had to be distributed between two lectures.

gratitude our best reward. And may the God of all power grant to us and to those in authority under us, strength to carry out these our wishes for the good of our people."

This Proclamation was read to the people of India by the first of Queen Victoria's Viceroys, Lord Canning of illustrious memory, on the 1st day of November, 1858, appropriately, as it seems to me, in the sacred city of Prayag near the confluence of Ganga and Yamuna. If the noble sentiments that breathed through this Proclamation had uniformly informed the government of this country by England the course of Indian politics would have been quite different from what it has actually been. Then would British and Indian opinion have been united as the Ganges and the Jumna are, in one stream, and loyalty and patriotism would have been synonymous terms. And the aspiration publicly expressed by the noblest of Viceroys would have become a fact, viz., that public opinion in India should be, as it was in England, the irresistible and unresisted master of government. Queen Victoria prayed to God for strength for her and her Government to act in accordance with the principles enunciated in her Proclamation. If a truly religious spirit had inspired the policies and measures of authority the British would have said to the Indians—" The government of your country is your affair, not ours. We have done our best to prepare you for the assumption of responsibility for the government of your own country and we now retire." And the Indians would have said in answer—"Yes, but we wish you to stay, not, it is true, as masters but as comrades in a common cause, on a footing of complete equality." It is the misfortune of this world that at least in politics authority is too apt to forget God and rule out of order the moral motive. The result is what we sorrowfully witness today—greater aloofness between Britain and India, less faith in the purposes of British statesmanship, a widely diffused feeling that the constitutional method, which is an appeal to reason, is not likely to achieve the aspiration of every Indian worthy of the name—Swaraj or the full rights of national self-government.

Raja Rammohun Roy

The foundations of the modern public life of India were first laid in Bengal by the great Raja Rammohun Roy. He led the movement of religious reform and founded the Brahma Samaj ; he took up the cause of India's women and was the pioneer of social reform. He initiated that process of the development of Bengali literature which has borne such rich fruit ; he took a leading part in the movement for the introduction of English education in India ; he took up the cause of political reform, advocated the separation of judicial and executive functions and was the first Indian to go to England to give evidence before a parliamentary committee. Lord Morley once remarked that there was no new question in Indian politics. This remark is illustrated by the reference which has been made to the separation of judicial from executive functions. More than a century has elapsed since the death of Rammohun Roy, yet this reform has not been effected. Rammohun Roy added to his other services by the establishment of a journal, perhaps the first which was conducted by an Indian. Rammohun Roy's activities were before the period to which these lectures relate ; as were those of the first public man in the western presidency of whom we have knowledge, Mr. Nowrosjee Faridoonjee. It was the latter's distinction to have been the teacher at school of the greatest of Indian patriots, Dadabhai Naoroji, styled by his countrymen with affection and reverence the Grand Old Man of India.

Dadabhai Naoroji

Dadabhai Naoroji began his public life at the age of 20 and ceaselessly toiled with a single-minded motive and a rare concentration of purpose for 61 long years. Born in 1825 when George IV was the King of England, Dadabhai Naoroji did not retire from public activities until the age of 81. His death in 1917 in his 92nd year marked the disappearance of an institution. The public life of India has been adorned by a galaxy of brilliant intellects and selfless patriots, but there has been none in our time comparable with Dadabhai Naoroji. He was the founder, in India and in England, of no fewer than thirty institutions, most of which had for their object the political advancement of the country, but some concerned themselves with social reform, in particular the education and emancipation of women. He founded the first girls' school in Bombay and he also founded the first newspaper and he was among the founders of the Indian National Congress. I had the rare good fortune of knowing him in his last years and a gentler soul I have never met. His very appearance inspired reverence. In the language of Mr. Lalmohun Ghose he filled his countrymen with "admiration, envy and despair". Mr. Gokhale said of him, "If ever there is the divine in man it is in Dadabhai."

The first public man of whom we know in the Madras presidency was Mr. Gazula Lakshmi Narasimhulu Chetty, who founded the Madras Native Association and the *Crescent* newspaper.

Other Public Men

Public men who first entered public life in the years before the birth of the Congress and later rose to eminence as all-India leaders included Mahadeo Govind Ranade, Badruddin Tyabji, Pherozeshah Merwanjee Mehta, Kashinath Trimbak Telang, Dinshaw Eduljee Wacha, Jhaverilal

Umiashankar Yajnik, Rahimtoolah Muhammad Sayani, Narayan Ganesh Chandavarkar and Bal Gangadhar Tilak in Bombay ; W. C. Bonnerjee, Manomohan Ghose, Surendranath Banerjea, Lalmohan Ghose, Ananda Mohan Bose and Kali Churn Banurji in Bengal ; the two Subramania Iyers (S. & G.), Ananda Charlu, Salem Ramaswami Mudaliar and C. Vijiaraghavachariar in Madras, and Pandit Madan Mohan Malaviya in the United Provinces.

British Indian Association, Calcutta

The earliest of our public organizations was the British Indian Association of Calcutta, an organization of the zemindars of Bengal, Bihar and Orissa. In the far-off years of which I am now speaking this Association was in its way a pioneer in political agitation. It was under its auspices that several famous men of Bengal took to public life and came into prominence. Among them were Harish Chandra Mukerji, the great editor of the Association's paper, the *Hindoo Patriot*, and his successor, Kristo Das Pal ; the great orator, Ram Gopal Ghosh; Raja Digambar Mitter, Maharajas Ramanath and Sir Jotendra Mohan Tagore, Maharaja Bahadur Sir Narendra Krishna, Raja Rajendra Narayan Deb Bahadur and Raja Rajendra Lall Mitra. Another very distinguished public man of those years in Bengal was the rev. K. M. Banerjee, perhaps the first as he was the greatest of Indian Christians to identify themselves with the national movement. But the British Indian Association being primarily a landlord organization, the need was felt of a more popular body and it was supplied by the Bengal National League, of which the principal founder was Babu Sisir Kumar Ghosh, the founder and first editor of the *Amrita Bazar Patrika*, renowned equally as publicist and spiritualist. This body was soon after superseded by the Indian Association, still in active existence, founded by Messrs. Surendranath Banerjea and Ananda Mohan Bose.

Bombay Presidency Association

In Bombay the corresponding organization was the Bombay Association, of which the leading figure was the famous jurist, Vishwanath Narayan Mandlik. This body was replaced some years later by the Bombay Presidency Association, with which the names of Sir Pherozeshah Mehta and Sir Dinshaw Wacha will for ever be inseparably associated. Poona, although it is in the presidency of Bombay, has always maintained its distinct individuality as the former capital of the Mahrattas, and in Poona Mahadeo Govind Ranade was the friend, philosopher and guide of an institution which for many years did the most notable service to the country, the Sarvajanik Sabha. Political differences among its members led to the formation in later years, again under the auspices of Mr. Ranade, of the Deccan Sabha. First the Sarvajanik Sabha and next the Deccan Sabha had the distinction of having Mr. Gokhale as secretary for several years. The quarterly *Journal* of the former, to which Mr. Ranade largely contributed, was the first and last of its kind. Its pages were full of information and instruction. In Madras the Native Association, to which reference has been made, gave place to the Mahajana Sabha.

Journalistic Activity

During this period also began journalistic activity among Indians. Besides the *Hindoo Patriot*, which has been mentioned, the *Indian Mirror*, the *Amrita Bazar Patrika*, the *Bengalee* and *Reis* and *Rayyat* were started in Bengal. Among the founders of the *Indian Mirror* was the celebrated Keshub Chunder Sen. Its first editor was Mr. Manomohan Ghose and later, it passed into the hands of Babu Norendro Nath Sen, who rendered distinguished service for many years. Babu Sisir Kumar Ghosh was succeeded as editor of the *Patrika* by his younger brother Babu Motilal Ghosh. It was changed from a Bengali into an English paper to escape the consequences of the Vernacular Press Act. The *Bengalee* was taken over from Mr. W. C. Bonnerjeee by Mr. Surendranath Banerjea. The mouths of journalists of today may water when they learn that the first printing press of the *Patrika* was purchased for Rs. 32, while the price at which the *Bengalee* was sold to its new proprietor was only Rs. 25 ![1] In Bombay Mr. Dadabhai Naoroji founded the *Voice of India* and Mr. Mandlik conducted *Native Opinion.* The *Indian Spectator* was Mr. Malabari's paper. Then, and for long afterwards, Mr. (now Sir Dinshaw) Wacha was a prolific writer in more papers than one. The *Indu Prakash* was in charge, first of Mr. Telang and next of Mr. (afterwards Sir Narayan) Chandavarkar. The *Kesari* was conducted, first by Mr. Agarkar and next by Mr. Tilak. The latter also edited the English weekly, the *Mahratta.* There were several other papers in Gujarati and Marathi. The most notable of journalistic events of that early period was the foundation of the *Hindu.* The name of its first and greatest editor, Mr. G. Subramania Iyer, will live as long as journalism exists. Pandit Ajodhia Nath founded the *Indian Herald* at Allahabad, but it was stopped after three years and the loss of a lakh of rupees. Sardar Dayal Singh Majithia gave the Punjab the *Tribune.*

Foundation of Universities

On the part of the Government the first act of progress after the direct assumption of sovereignty by the Queen was the foundation of the three universities of Calcutta, Bombay and Madras. This was an act of courageous and farsighted

1. I had to pay Rs. 300 in 1899 for the good-will of the *Vizag Spectator*.

statesmanship and, coming as it did on the morrow of the mutiny it might be interpreted as a message of hope to the people of India and a symbol of the good will of England. As a parallel case might be mentioned the appeal of Lord Kitchener for generous public support for an educational institution at Khartoum, the Gordon Memorial College, after his resounding victory at Omdurman in 1898. This was England's way. It is illustrated by a conversation between the great Mountstuart Elphinstone when he was Governor of Bombay and Lt.-Gen. Briggs, who served under him at the time of the Mahratta crisis. "On my observing in a corner of his tent one day" says that officer, "a pile of printed Marathi books I asked him what they were meant for." "To educate the natives," said he ; "but it is our high road back to Europe." "Then" I replied, "I wonder you as Governor of Bombay have set it on foot". He answered, "We are bound, under all circumstances, to do our duty to them." And Macaulay said that this same path of duty was also "the path of wisdom, of national prosperity and of national honour".

Indian Councils Act, 1861

Three years later the Indian Councils Act of 1861 was passed. The Legislative Council of the Governor-General was first established a few years before the mutiny but its membership was limited to officials among whom, we may note with curiosity, was the Chief Justice of Bengal. By the Act of 1861 provision was made for the inclusion of a few nominated nonofficials to the council. This was followed by the establishment of similar councils in the three presidencies. The beginnings of provincial financial decentralization and of local self-government marked the viceroyalty of Lord Mayo. But in 1871 was inserted in the Penal Code the now historic section 124A providing for the punishment of the offence of sedition. And in the time of Lord Lytton were passed the Vernacular Press Act and the Arms Act. The former was repealed by his successor, Lord Ripon, but the latter continues to be on the statute-book, only with some changes in the Act or in the rules made thereunder. The six years 1874-1880 were a period of political reaction. The second Afghan war was wantonly embarked upon, for the supposed benefit of England but at the cost of the Indian taxpayer—except for an inadequate contribution of £5 millions from the British Treasury made subsequently at the instance of Mr. Gladstone.

Indian Civil Service

In the same period the rules regulating the recruitment of the Indian Civil Service were altered to the prejudice of Indians. When the recruitment of this service by competition was substituted for the old Haileybury system India's great friend, John Bright, criticized the measure on the ground that it afforded few facilities for Indians themselves to join the service of their own country. When it was argued in defence that there was no race exclusion John Bright retorted that they might as well say that conditions were absolutely equal as between Englishmen and Indians, only the Indian competitors must be 8 feet 6 inches in height ! The holding of the examination exclusively in England was a curious commentary on section 87 of the Charter Act of 1833 and the Royal Proclamation of 1858, which promised equality of opportunity to Indians. In forwarding the former to the Governor-General in Council the Court of Directors of the East India Company authoritatively told him that its meaning was that from that time onward there was to be no governing caste in India. Alack for the futility of human hopes ! As the result of strong agitation by Dadabhai Naoroji an Act was passed in 1870 by which a limited number of Indians was to be admitted to the I. C. S. by nomination. The rules under the Act were not made until 1878, and a very few men were actually appointed. This (the Statutory Civil Service) was abolished as the result of the Public Service Commission of 1886-1888 and in its place were constituted the provincial civil services. In spite of the tremendous disadvantage that the examination was held only in London a few Indians succeeded in obtaining entrance into the I. C. S., the earliest of them being Mr. Satyendranath Tagore, son of Devendranath and brother of Dr. Rabindranath Tagore. Among those who followed were Messrs. R. C. Dutt and Surendranath Banerjea and Sir K. G. Gupta. And among the failures was Mr. Manomohan Ghose. But the success of even a very few Indians so alarmed the generous-hearted British Government, colour-blind and free from race prejudice, that the age limit was reduced from 23 to 19 thereby making it all but impossible for Indians to compete. Lord Lytton said in an official dispatch to the Secretary of State "we have broken to the heart the hopes held out to the ear", and he added that England had acted in the " least straightforward " manner. The Vernacular Press Act and this reduction of the age limit for the I. C. S. led the newly founded Indian Association to depute to England Mr. Lalmohan Ghose for agitation on these two subjects. Mr. Lalmohan Ghose was just 30 when he proceeded to England on this mission. The first public meeting he addressed was in Willis's Rooms and under the chairmanship of no less a man than John Bright. This inexperienced young man of 30 made a speech of which John Bright said, "I will not spoil the effect of the magnificent oration we have heard by any feeble words of my own." And of John Bright it was said that but for him Gladstone would have been the greatest orator of England—Gladstone, whose style of oratory was described by Lord Rosebery as " a rolling river of majestic diction". Mr. Lalmohan Ghose at the instance of John Bright was able to see Gladstone and enlist his support. The result was a debate in the House of Commons, in which Gladstone took part and said that the Vernacular Press Act was a disgrace to the Government. When Gladstone became Prime Minister with Lord Ripon as Viceroy the Act was repealed. And subsequently the age limit for entrance into the Civil Service was also raised. Mr. Lalmohan Ghose made such impression on British audiences by his eloquence that "the bronzed orator" as he was called, drew vast audiences wherever he was announced to appear on the platform, won the admiration of such men as Lord Rosebery and Mr. Joseph Chamberlain and was twice selected as a Liberal candidate for Parliament. He did not succeed, but his failure paved the way for the election six years later of Dadabhai Naoroji. In later years Mr. Lalmohan Ghose took an inconspicuous part in public activities. He only appeared on the Congress platform at Calcutta except for his presidentship at Madras in 1903. It may be recalled that in his brilliant address to that Congress he described the "Curzonoration" Durbar of the beginning of that year as "a pompous pageantry to a perishing people". His last appearance on the Congress platform was in 1906, when he made his last brilliant speech in proposing a vote of thanks to the president, Dadabhai Naoroji, and eloquently vindicated constitutional agitation against its new critics. Of all the orators whom it has been my privilege to hear, I have no hesitation in according the first place (along with Mrs. Besant) to Mr. Lalmohan Ghose, who was known as the John Bright of India.

Lord Ripon

The policy of the Government underwent a radical change with the advent of the Liberal party to power in England. Incidentally, may I suggest to the younger generation of students of Indian politics that their study would not be complete unless they took in concurrently British and Indian politics ? On this subject I would commend a small but instructive book by Mr. R. C. Dutt entitled "England and India, 1785-1885". In that book Mr. Dutt brought out period by period how the currents of policy in England and India ran in parallel streams. Lord Ripon, who succeeded Lord Lytton in 1880, was easily the noblest of Viceroys. A truly pious man, he never had any use for subterfuge in politics. He held tenaciously by Burke's doctrine that "what is morally wrong cannot be politically right" and always acted in complete accord with this teaching. What he was actually able to do during the four years of his viceroyalty might not have been much, but the recorded achievement is a very unfair index to the intentions and efforts of that high-souled statesman. The difficulties by which he was surrounded must never be lost sight of. He laid the foundations of local self-government, a very modest thing as we would be inclined to say today, but a by no means easy task in those days. He was answered by the passive resistance of the bureaucracy at every step. And in the practice of this art of passive resistance Mahatma Gandhi himself must take a back seat behind the organized bureaucracy of India. I know no class of men who are more skilled than the permanent officials in defeating reform in detail. In his attempt to purge the Criminal Procedure Code of provisions which made unabashed race distinctions—the measure introduced in this behalf is known to history as the Ilbert Bill after the name of the then Law Member—Lord Ripon encountered the most furious opposition from his countrymen in India while he got insufficient support from the Secretary of State. If Lord Ripon was the beloved of the people of India he was the target of unceasing and malignant attacks from his own countrymen. He left India a year before his time in a spirit of sheer helplessness. His viceroyalty most forcibly illustrated that perpetual conflict of interest, of opinion, of purpose between the people of India and the temporary British sojourners in the country, of which first Burke and then Mill had to take notice. This had to be deplored by a predecessor of Lord Ripon's a score of years before his time. Sir John (afterwards Lord) Lawrence wrote :

> The difficulty in the way of the Government of India acting fairly in these matters is immense. If anything is done, or attempted to be done, to help the natives, a general howl is raised, which reverberates in England, and finds sympathy and support there. I feel quite bewildered sometimes what to do. Every one is, in the abstract, for justice, moderation and such like excellent qualities; but when one comes to apply such principles so as to affect anybody's interests, then a change comes over them. (Letter to Sir Erskine Perry, member, India Council.)

Lord Lytton's most reactionary regime—there is a difference of opinion whether Lord Lytton or Lord Curzon should get the bottom place among Viceroys—nearly filled the Indian public men of that day with dismay bordering on despair, so much so that the great Dadabhai Naoroji himself, in whose breast, if in any, hope shone like a sacred pillar of fire, almost thought of abandoning political activities. It was during that time that he became Dewan of Baroda, but he relinquished the position in less than a year. Lord Ripon's viceroyalty kindled a new hope and proved a great stimulus to the revival of public activities in intensified measure. One of the indirect results of his viceroyalty was the Indian National Congress founded a year after his departure.

State of Politics and Public Life

At this point may be summed up the state of politics and public life in India in the period between the Mutiny and the foundation of the National Congress. The policy of the Government alternated between modest progress and strong reaction. It depended very much, not upon the force of Indian opinion as there was no organized Indian opinion but upon the changing policies of the British Government and the British Parliament. There was a succession of more or less good Viceroys beginning with Canning and ending with Ripon—they included Lawrence, Mayo and Northbrook—but there was also Lord Lytton, who tried to undo as much as possible of what his predecessors had done. If on the affirmative side the establishment of universities was the greatest thing done by the Government after the Mutiny, on the negative side there was the fresh combination of executive and judicial functions which had been separated before it, there was the Vernacular Press Act, there was the forward frontier policy involving disastrous financial consequences to India, there was the Arms Act and there were the repeated attempts to frustrate the aim of Indians to enter the superior services of the country—I mean civil as there was no thought at all of their admission to the commissioned ranks of the army. But on the credit side must also be mentioned the Councils Act of 1861, the steady progress of education and the introduction of local self-governing institutions. The majority of nonofficial members nominated to the councils answered the description which our longer experience of that species enables us to give of them. The orator of the Congress described the councils of those days as "gilded shams" and their nominated members as "magnificent nonentities". A curious incident is deserving of mention. The same nominated nonofficial members who voted for the Vernacular Press Act under Lord Lytton voted for its repeal under Lord Ripon! Their constituency was Government House and they were true to it. But it should not be thought that there were no exceptions to this inglorious rule. There were bound to be, for they included

Vishwanath Narayan Mandlik, and in after years, before there was the semblance of election there were some nominated members of the type of Dadabhai Naoroji, Ranade, Telang, Tyabji and Mehta in Bombay; Kristo Das Pal and Raja Pearey Mohan Mukerji in Bengal; Sir S. Subramania Iyer in Madras, and the late Pandit Ajodhia Nath in the United Provinces (then called the North-Western Provinces). When the import duty on Lancashire textile goods was abolished in the name of free trade one of the members was Mandlik. His protest having proved unavailing, he appeared the next day in Council in the homespun country cloth now known as *khaddar* and he frankly said that he did so as a political protest. Mandlik was not the man to disguise his feelings. Famous as a jurist, he was not less distinguished for independence. He did what he wanted to do and he openly proclaimed why he did it. But it should not be thought from examples like this, which necessarily are few and far between, that there is political virtue in the system of nomination any more than it would be right to discredit the system of popular election because of the many abuses that crept into it and of the many unworthy men who managed to succeed at the polls. On the part of our countrymen the foundations of organized public life were firmly laid in the three presidencies, but more particularly in Bombay and Bengal. The greatest of leaders was Dadabhai Naoroji and under him grew up Mahadeo Govind Ranade and Pherozeshah Merwanji Mehta. Others who came under his influence included Badruddin Tyabji, W. C. Bonnerjee, Manomohan Ghose and R. C. Dutt. The greatest figure in Bengal public life during the major part of that period was Kristo Das Pal, who wielded great influence through the columns of the *Hindoo Patriot*, of which he was the editor. Provincial political associations were established on a firm footing and the way was paved for the united national effort that followed in the second period which began with the establishment of the Congress.

CHAPTER II[1]

II

1885—1905

THE CONGRESS (FIRST TWENTY YEARS)

The idea of a national assemblage for definitely political ends was conceived by a number of leading men and the idea materialized in the year 1885. The name first proposed was the Indian National Conference and Poona was selected as the venue of its first session. Due to an outbreak of cholera it had to be changed to Bombay and the first Congress was held in that city on December 28, 1885, in Gokuldas Tejpal High School. It was a small body of picked men who elected themselves as delegates. The President was Mr. W. C. Bonnerjee, and among those who took part in the deliberations were Dadabhai Naoroji, Pherozeshah Mehta, Kashinath Trimbak Telang, Jhaverilal Yajnik, Dinshaw Edulji Wacha, R. M. Sayani, Gopal Ganesh Agarkar and Narayan Ganesh Chandavarkar of Bombay; Sir S. Subramania Iyer, Dewan Bahadur Ragoonath Rao, P. Anandacharlu, G. Subramania Iyer, P. Rungiah Naidu and M. Viraraghavachariar of Madras, and Babu Norendro Nath Sen of Calcutta. A young man of 22 who travelled all the way from Lucknow to Bombay, unknown and undistinguished, was Babu Ganga Prasad Varma, who lived to be one of the greatest devotees of the Congress and of the Motherland during the 28 years that he lived after the first Congress. Addressing as I do an Andhra audience under the auspices of the Andhra University I think I may mention that

1. This was delivered as a part of the first lecture.

Andhra districts and Andhra people were represented at the first Congress by Mr. S. P. Narasimhulu Naidu of Coimbatore, Rai Bahadur A. Sabhapati Mudaliar of Bellary, Dewan Bahadur P. Kesava Pillai of Gooty and Rao Saheb Singaraju Venkatasubbarayudu Pantulu Garu of Masulipatam (whose name Mr. Badruddin Tyabji said he would not venture to pronounce). Among the founders of the Congress the only survivor is Sir Dinshaw Wacha, living in retirement but happily hale and hearty in his 92nd year[1]. Most conspicuous of all who assisted at the birth of the Congress and who afterwards became its life and soul for six years was Allan Octavian Hume, known as the father of the Congress. Mr. Hume became its general secretary, travelled all over India unfailingly year after year and did everything that man could do to spread and popularize the gospel of the Congress, spending on the work every time and all the time his own money. He was a man with a dynamic personality and galvanized into life the most inert of men who came into contact with him. It is worthy of mention as illustrating the latitude allowed to officials in those years that the resolutions of the first Congress were settled at a private meeting held at the residence of Principal Wordsworth of Elphinstone College and attended by other officials who included Sir William Wedderburn, Mr. Ranade, and Rai Bahadur Lala Baij Nath of the province of Agra. Mr. Ranade went farther and took part in the deliberations of the open session. In further illustration of this point may be mentioned that Mr. Ranade as a nominated official member of the Bombay Council once or twice put questions like nonofficial elected members, and that in the Bengal Council of the same period two official members, Sir Henry Cotton and

1. Sir Dinshaw Wacha has since passed away, to the great regret of his numerous friends and admirers, Indian and English.

Mr. R. C. Dutt, at least once voted with the elected members against the Government. And Sir Henry Cotton was the chief secretary to Government! But in 1890 there was a little storm in a tea cup.

Congress and Officials

When the Congress met in Calcutta in that year the usual invitations sent to the members of the Viceroy's household were returned on the ground that officials could not attend a political assemblage. The misunderstanding was, however, soon cleared and no such difficulty was again created. When the Congress met at Madras in 1887 the Governor, Lord Connemara, helped the reception committee with supplies from Government House. But in 1888, at Allahabad Sir Auckland Colvin made up his mind that the Congress should not be held and he created no end of difficulties in the way of the reception committee securing a place where to erect the Congress camp. The Congress of that year as well as of 1892 was held on the extensive grounds of Lowther Castle, purchased by the then Maharaja of Darbhanga, a great friend of the Congress, and since known as Darbhanga Castle. When the Congress met at Nagpur in 1891 the chief commissioner, Mr. A. P. (afterwards Sir Antony and next Lord) Macdonnell publicly declared that he thought no worse and no better of any man for joining or not joining the Congress. Difficulties were again placed in the way of the Congress reception committee at Lucknow in 1899 by an over-zealous deputy commissioner but he was overruled and facilities were given to the committee by the Lieutenant-Governor, Sir Antony Macdonnell. In 1914, at Madras the Governor, Lord Pentland, himself attended the Congress while two years later, at Lucknow the Lieutenant-Governor, Sir James (now Lord) Meston improved upon the example set by Lord Pentland and addressed the

Congress. Going back to 1888, a year of difficulties for the Congress crowned by the most interesting and one of the most successful of sessions, Lord Dufferin emptied the vials of his wrath on the devoted head of the Congress in his speech at St. Andrews Dinner at Calcutta. I would recommend to the younger generation of students of Indian politics a perusal of the controversies of that time in which prominently figured such masters of dialectics as Lord Dufferin and Sir Auckland Colvin on the official side and Messrs. Hume, Norton and Telang on the Congress side.

The First Congress

The first Congress gave its attention to a number of important subjects which are still live issues in Indian politics. The first resolution of the first Congress, which advocated a royal commission to inquire into Indian administration, was moved by one who made public life in Madras, principally through the *Hindu*, Mr. G. Subramania Iyer. That Congress advocated the reform and expansion of legislative councils and simultaneous examinations for the Indian Civil Service. In view of the present position of Burma in relation to India it is instructive to recall that the first Congress on the motion of Sir Pherozeshah Mehta protested against the annexation of Upper Burma and urged that, if it must be annexed, Burma should be treated as a crown colony and should not be made a burden upon Indian revenues. But it was made a burden, and after the Indian taxpayer paid the cost of the three Burmese wars and financed the government of Burma during its many years of deficit that country is now about to be separated from India[1] without adequate financial reparation and with no guarantee that the Indians who are settled there will receive just and equal treatment. In fact Sir Harcourt Butler, when he was

1. This has since been done.

Lieutenant-Governor of Burma, was allowed by the Government of India to place on the statute-book legislative and financial measures which reduced the position of Indians almost as if Burma were another Kenya.

The Second Congress

When the Congress met in Calcutta in the following year, this time under the presidency of Dadabhai Naoroji, delegates were elected by public bodies and public meetings, and their number rose from about 70 at the first session to 436 in the second session. It met on two days in the hall of the British Indian Association, and as it was found inadequate, on the following two days in the Town Hall. Among the acquisitions of that year were Raja Rajendra Lall Mitra, chairman of the reception committee, who shared with Sir Ramakrishna Bhandarkar the distinction of being India's greatest oriental scholar, Surendranath Banerjea and Pandit Madan Mohan Malaviya.

The Third Congress

The Congress grew from strength to strength year by year. At Madras in 1887 it had its first Muslim president in the illustrious person of Mr. (afterwards Justice) Badruddin Tyabji and its reception committee had the rare honour of having for its chairman the greatest of Indian statesmen, Raja Sir T. Madhava Rao, who described the Congress as "the soundest triumph of British administration and a crown of glory to the British nation". The number of delegates rose to 607. Among the acquisitions of this year besides Sir T. Madhava Rao and Mr. Badruddin Tyabji were Mr. Eardley Norton, Pandit Bishan Narayan Dar, Sir Sankaran Nair, Mr. John Adam, Mr. Salem Ramaswami Mudaliar, and from this city Mr. (afterwards Sir) B. N. Sarma. As a matter of local interest

I may be permitted to mention that among the illustrious personages who contributed to the funds of that session of the Congress and who attended it as a visitor was one whose name cannot be mentioned, at least in this part of the country, without respect and admiration—Maharaja Sir Ananda Gajapati Raj of Vizianagram—the incarnation of patience, the embodiment of charity and a son who acted and lived in the faith नमातु: परदैवतम्—a very Prince Charming as he was called. It may not be generally known today that that illustrious prince, the patron of not a few of us of the older generation at Vizianagram, was a great friend of Surendranath Banerjea in Bengal and G. Subramania Iyer in Madras, and the home of the Indian Association was his gift. I have mentioned Mr. Eardley Norton as being among the acquisitions to the Congress of the year 1887. It will add, perhaps needlessly, to the length of these lectures if I overburdened them with citations from notable speeches of the earlier years of the Congress and I propose therefore to avoid them as far as possible. But an exception may be made in favour of one passage of Mr. Norton's first great speech. What is more familiar to us in these days than prosecutions for sedition? It appears that Mr. Norton was stigmatized by a fellow-countryman as a "veiled seditionist" for the offence of joining the Congress. Mr. Norton was not the man to take anything lying down and he answered his critic in a passage which deserves to be remembered for long. He said :

> If it be sedition, gentlemen, to rebel against all wrong, if it be sedition to insist that the people should have a fair share in the administration of their own country and affairs, if it be sedition to resist class tyranny, to raise my voice against oppression, to mutiny against injustice, to insist upon a hearing before sentence, to uphold the liberties of the individual, to vindicate our common right to gradual but ever advancing reform—if this be

sedition, I am right glad to be called a 'seditionist', and doubly, aye trebly glad when I look around me today to know and feel I am ranked as one among such a magnificent array of seditionists.

The Fourth Congress

The Congress continued to grow in strength. It aroused more opposition in 1888 than in the previous two years. There was a combination of Sir Auckland Colvin and Sir Syed Ahmad. The latter gave a definite lead to his co-religionists to keep aloof from the Congress and founded what he called the Anglo-Muslim Defence Association. The opposition, however, produced, contrary to the intention and expectation of its authors, a very wholesome effect on the public mind and the session held at the end of the year was more successful than any of the three preceding sessions. Pandit Ajodhia Nath, the lion of the United Provinces, was at the head of the reception committee and roused the people by his fiery eloquence. He was ready to hold the Congress at any cost, wholly at his own expense if necessary. His death about three years later at the early age of 51 was a national misfortune. The number of delegates in that year rose to 1248. Nearly all the leading men were present and took part in the debates. The report of that session may be commended for study as a political education by itself. At that session the Congress had its first British president in the person of Mr. George Yule, a leading merchant of Calcutta. He delivered a remarkable address which may still be read with profit. He pointed out that all movements of the nature of the Congress passed through several phases as they ran their course.

The first [he said] is one of ridicule. That is followed, as the movement progresses, by one of abuse which is usually succeeded by partial concession and misapprehension of aim, accompanied by warnings against taking 'big jumps into the unknown'. The final stage of all is a substantial adoption of the object of the movement with some expression of surprise that it was not adopted before. These various phases overlap each other, but between the first and last the distinction is complete.

The Congress of the following year was still larger. It met at Bombay under the presidency of Sir William Wedderburn. It was attended by Charles Bradlaugh. By a curious coincidence the number of delegates in that year 1889 was exactly 1889. Mr. Gokhale joined the Congress for the first time in that year and made a speech which led to a prophecy that he was a future president of the Congress. His success was instantaneous and comparable to Mr. Asquith's when he made his maiden speech in the House of Commons which made political prophets declare "here is a future Prime Minister". At the conclusion of the Congress addresses were presented to Mr. Bradlaugh on behalf of all parts of the country. Mr. Bradlaugh said in the course of a memorable oration: "For whom should I work if not for the people? Born of the people, trusted by the people, I will die of the people and I know no geographical or race limitations."

The Fifth Congress

In those years the foremost subject before the Congress year after year was the expansion and reform of the legislative councils. After the passing of the Indian Councils Act of 1892 pride of place was given to a resolution on simultaneous examinations for the Indian Civil Service in England and in India. The House of Commons carried a resolution in this behalf in 1893 on the motion of Mr. Herbert Paul, but the Governments in England and India combined to frustrate that resolution and reduced it to a "scrap of paper". The Congress of 1893, which was held at Lahore, was rendered memorable by the second presidency of Dadabhai Naoroji, who in the previous year was elected a member of the House of Commons. He was the first Indian M. P. He was succeeded three years later by another Parsi, Sir Muncherjee

Subsequent Sessions

Bhownaggree, who however did not identify himself with the Indian national movement. After him there was one more Indian member, also a Parsi, Mr. Saklatwala. There have been no more Indian members of the House of Commons although several, among them Mr. W. C. Bonnerjee, more than once stood for election. There was however one Indian member of the House of Lords, the late Lord Sinha. Dadabhai Naoroji received in India from the moment of his landing at Bombay right to the moment of his sailing back for England, at every place which he visited and on the platform of almost every railway station where his train halted, a reception unprecedented until then, and equalled, during many years afterwards, only by the reception accorded to him at Calcutta thirteen years later when he again came to preside over the Congress.[1] That was a reception which, in the language of Surendranath Banerjea, "princes and kings may envy but cannot command". The Congress ran on an even course until the year 1905. There was not a single question of public importance which did not engage its attention and the views embodied in its resolutions on various subjects year after year testified to the political wisdom of the leaders of the movement.

Indian Councils Act, 1892

Thirty-one years after the Act of 1861, and as the result of years of agitation, continuously by the Congress for six years during which two deputations visited England, the Indian Councils Act of 1892 was passed. It made what at this day must appear but meagre concessions but which at that time could not be disregarded as being either unimportant or unsubstantial. The number of members was

1. In recent years political receptions have become a feature of public life and Mahatma Gandhi has become the hero and darling of his countrymen.

increased and provision was made for the nomination of some members on the recommendation of statutory local bodies, universities and chambers of commerce, though the principle of election was not recognized in terms. The right of interpellation was given, but without the right of supplementary questions. Councils could discuss the budget in general terms, but no motions of reduction could be made. Neither could members move resolutions. The rules under the Act were utterly unsatisfactory—as such rules have almost always been—and gave rise to agitation. When the Bill was before Parliament, both the Prime Minister and the leader of the Opposition (Lord Salisbury and Mr. Gladstone) averred that real, living representation should be given to the people. The rules did precisely the contrary. But, strictly limited as were the opportunities of members, not a few of them did make themselves useful to the people, while some of them highly distinguished themselves by their parliamentary ability. The greatest of them by common consent were Sir Pherozeshah Mehta and Mr. Gokhale. Among others who deserve mention even at this distance of time were Surendranath Banerjea (whose work on the Calcutta Municipal Bill cannot be forgotten by those who witnessed it) and Ananda Mohan Bose in Bengal, Messrs. C. Vijiaraghavachariar and N. Subbarau Pantulu in Madras, Sir Chimanlal Setalvad and Sir Gokuldas Parekh in Bombay, and Pandit Madan Mohan Malaviya in the United Provinces. It would be a mistake to belittle the value of the work of these and other members because it did not always or often bear fruit. For it is certain that if the majority of them had been failures ; if they had betrayed a lack of capacity or of a sense of responsibility, if they had not acted in the best interests of the people there would have been no Morley-Minto councils in after-years. The working hypothesis of earnest public men can only be that, as the father of the Congress said, honest work unselfishly done never fails in the long run.

Lord Lansdowne

During the period of review India had the misfortune of having Viceroys manifestly out of sympathy with Indian aspirations. Lord Dufferin's successor, the Marquess of Lansdowne, was responsible for what was known as "the crime of June 26, 1893", when at a single sitting of his Legislative Council held at Simla and in the absence of every elected Indian member a measure was passed closing the Indian mints to the free coinage of silver. Our currency and exchange troubles began about that time and have not yet come to an end after the lapse of 42 years, and threaten to continue under the coming constitution which denies power to the so-called responsible government of the future to deal with the subject except with the previous sanction of the Governor-General acting as the subordinate of the Secretary of State.

Exchange Compensation Allowance

On the same day was passed another selfish and objectionable measure by which what was known as "exchange compensation allowance" was granted to British officers in India. This and the many other allowances given to them—they were enumerated by Sir Abdur Rahim in his Minority Report of the Islington Commission on the Civil Services of India (1915) and have since been added to still more as the result of the Lee Commission of 1923—were a virtual addition to their very high and altogether excessive salaries, at the cost of an impoverished people. Speaking at the Congress of the following year (1894), a Punjab patriot, the late Lala Murlidhar, said :

"It is easier for a camel to pass through the eye of a needle than for a rich man to enter the Kingdom of Heaven." If that precept were to be taken in its literal sense and accepted as Gospel truth, then I submit there is no happier country than India and there are no happier people than the Indians. You should pity the rich people of England for the vast treasures of wealth they have hoarded,.....and you should thank heaven that you have been placed in this desirable position, that the doors of heaven have been opened to you while they have been shut against all the people of Europe........ Have not the officials undergone a considerable amount of sacrifice by throwing open the doors of heaven to you, compensating themselves therefor by the so-called Exchange Compensation Allowance?" [1]

Lord Elgin

Lord Lansdowne's successor, Lord Elgin, was a huge failure. He went to Jubbulpur in the autumn of 1896 when famine was so raging in the province that, in the language of the subsequent Famine Commission, "people died like flies", and congratulated the people upon the prosperity of the Central Provinces right to the gates of Jubbulpur! His Government embarked upon the costly and extensive transfrontier military operations of 1895 and 1897 and involved India in huge financial loss. And after having sanctioned the political repression of 1897 and placed on the statute-book the legislative measures of 1898 to which reference will presently be made, he closed his undistinguished Indian career with a speech to the United Services Club of Simla, in which he openly made the unabashed declaration that "India was conquered by the sword and by the sword it shall be held". In after years, when Lord Elgin found himself Secretary of State for the Colonies he sanctioned measures for which our countrymen settled in South Africa had no reason to thank him. He was a good man and an honest man but manifestly incompetent. He confessed to Mr. Ananda Charlu, a great friend of his, that he knew nothing about India and would be a fool if he did not allow himself to be guided by his advisers.

---

1 This paragraph is an addition.

In the autumn of 1896 plague made its first appearance and famine also broke out. The
1897 following year was a year of disasters.
India was afflicted in that year by famine, plague, earthquake, war, repression. In fact, in the language of Mr. Ranade it appeared as if the seven plagues had been let loose upon India. The administration of plague measures, to which the people were unaccustomed and which caused much discomfort and misery, was carried out with benevolent intentions it is true, but with a rigour which led to breaches of the peace in more centres than one. At Poona the dissatisfaction grew so intense that on the night of the Queen's birthday the (I. C. S.) officer in charge of those measures, Mr. Rand, was murdered on his way back from Government House. With him was killed another officer, Lt. Ayerst. This combined blunder and crime so angered the Government that they embarked upon a campaign of organized repression. They acted on the assumption that the murder was the result of a conspiracy. But Mr. W. H. Crowe, then sessions judge of Poona and afterwards an acting judge of the Bombay High Court, who tried the accused (the Chapekar brothers) and sentenced them for that crime, declared in his charge to the jury that he had specially looked into any possible evidence of conspiracy but found none. Two brothers, the Sardars Natu, were deported under the Bombay Regulation XXV of 1827 promulgated for quite different purposes when India was still in an unsettled condition under the British. Mr. Tilak and a number of other publicists were prosecuted for sedition and sentenced to long terms of imprisonment. A new definition of the word "disaffection" occurring in sec. 124-A was given by the trying judge, Mr. Justice (afterwards Sir Arthur) Strachey, *viz.*, that it meant "absence of affection", and on

the basis of this obviously wrong definition Mr. Tilak was convicted by a majority of the jury and sentenced to rigorous imprisonment for eighteen months. Press committees were established in the Bombay presidency to control the publications in newspapers. Towards the close of the year bills were introduced in the Viceroy's Legislative Council to stiffen still more the already wide language in which section 124-A was drawn, to insert a new section—sec. 153-A—which has since been employed as a convenient handmaid of sec. 124-A, to deal with embitterment of relations between one community and another, and to provide for the punishment of persons who uttered outside India words which might be considered by the Government to constitute a political offence. At the same time it was proposed to amend the Criminal Procedure Code by the insertion of sec. 108 so as to enable magistrates to deal with persons alleged to be offenders under sec. 124-A or sec. 153-A in the same manner in which bad characters—real or alleged—could be disposed of under sec. 110. The Post Office Act was to be amended so as to empower postmasters to detain in transit postal articles which they might suspect contained matter of a seditious character. These bills were passed into law early in 1898 notwithstanding nation-wide opposition, which was led inside the Legislative Council by no less a man than the patriotic Maharaja Sir Lakshmeshwar Singh Bahadur of Darbhanga, to whom reference has been made. I have a personal recollection of those events, and can say that the opinion generally prevalent at the time was that the Government of Bombay were panic-stricken and the Government of India took advantage of the situation to deprive the people of some of their meagre rights. The Chitpavan Brahmans of the Deccan were political suspects as they were full of the glories of Sivaji and the

Peishwas, while Mr. Tilak by his personality and through his *Kesari* had already become a formidable antagonist. The Government's main source of information was the police. Ignorance and its foster-child, fear unnerved the Government of Lord Sandhurst and they went on acting as if they were confronted by something like organized revolt. Indian publicists were not alone in thinking that the Government of Bombay lost their head. Sir Antony Macdonnell, then Lieutenant-Governor of the United Provinces, remarked to Pandit Bishan Narayan Dar at the time, "What is this talk of unrest? Let them send me to Bombay and I shall restore quiet in a fortnight." While the system was, is and is likely to remain bad, the personality of the ruler does make a difference, as was shown ten years later in the Punjab, and twelve years later still by the difference in methods and results between that province under Sir Michael O'Dwyer and the United Provinces under Sir Harcourt Butler.

Lord Curzon

While plague continued to devastate the land with increasing severity and became the parent of regrettable political developments, a more severe famine than that of 1896-97 again afflicted the country in 1899-1900. Lord Curzon came out as Viceroy towards the close of 1898 and for seven long years inflicted upon the country in almost breathless succession one contentious measure after another to which the people took the strongest exception. He did some good things, it is true, but the dominant note struck throughout the period was that India was and must remain a "possession" of England, that England's imperial grip over India should be tightened and that no political advance should be thought of. His educational policy, which began with the forcing upon unwilling universities of Lee-Warner's "Citizen of India" as a text-book and ended with the passing of the Indian Universities Act of 1904, was interpreted by the people as an expression of the British Government's dissatisfaction with the political results of the diffusion of English education among Indians.[1] Lord Curzon's last utterance on education was a notorious address to the Convocation of Calcutta University in 1905, in which he libelled the people of India as having no regard for truth, and not content with this, went farther and had the boldness to say that truth had never been an Indian ideal. The most ironic comment on this was furnished by Sister Nivedita in the *Amrita Bazar Patrika* in the form of quotations from one of Lord Curzon's books in which he publicly confessed that he had told untruths to the Dowager Empress of China in order to impress her the more with his importance. Lord Curzon sent an expedition to Tibet, of course at the expense of Indian revenues. His crowning achievement was the partition of Bengal, which rightly exasperated the people of that province. This had repercussions which are felt to this day. When Lord Curzon suddenly left India, almost like a thief in the night, in the latter part of 1905 he left the country seething with discontent from end to end. And while he sowed the wind the whirlwind had to be reaped by his successor.

Secretaries of State

During the same period it was a further misfortune of India that she had Secretaries of State who vied with the Viceroys in making things worse all around. There was Sir Henry Fowler (afterwards Viscount Wolverhampton), a

1. For an exposure of the policy then in the ascendant and an exposition of principles that ought to guide policy, Sir Gooroo Dass Banerjee's Minute of Dissent affixed to the Report of the Indian Universities Commission of 1902, may be strongly commended. It has not been excelled by anything since written.

"Liberal" Secretary of State who could not have been more tory if he had called himself one. He was succeeded by Lord George Hamilton and the change was for us like unto jumping from the frying pan into the fire. If Sir Henry Fowler chastised India with whips, Lord George Hamilton chastised her with scorpions. One who was more completely out of sympathy with even the most modest of Indian national aspirations could with difficulty be discovered. For eight years did he stick to office and those years were for India one long drawn out agony. Lord George Hamilton was succeeded by Mr. St. John Brodrick (now the Earl of Midleton) for no other reason than that he had been so colossal a failure as Secretary of State for War that he had to be removed from that office. The political complexion of this Secretary of State could be seen from the two facts, first that he proposed that Indian revenues should bear a part of the cost of the British garrison in South Africa and secondly, that he sanctioned Lord Curzon's scheme of the partition of Bengal. Some of the provincial governors of that time were hardly better. They included such men as Lord Harris in Bombay, Sir Charles Crosthwaite in the United Provinces, and Sir Charles Elliott and Sir Alexander Mackenzie in Bengal.

Indians in South Africa

A subject which first came to the fore during this period must be mentioned in view of the aggravated dimensions it has since assumed. It is the oppression of our countrymen settled in South Africa and other parts of the empire. The first time the Congress was called upon to deal with this subject was in 1894 at Madras. By 1896 it had already become so acute that a young Indian barrister who, having gone to South Africa in a case was persuaded to stay on there for the service of his helpless and oppressed countrymen, came on a special mission to India to interest the Congress and Indian public men in their cause. He repeated his visit five years later on the same mission. Of that young Indian barrister a great deal has to be said, but not just yet.

British Committee of the Congress.

A few words should be said here of an organization that came into being during this period and proved to be a potent agency in the furtherance of India's cause in England. It was the British Committee of the Indian National Congress. It was the successor of the Indian Political Agency conducted by Mr. William Digby. Sir William Wedderburn was its chairman and its other leading members included Dadabhai Naoroji, A. O. Hume, W. S. Caine, Samuel Smith, W. C. Bonnerjee and Herbert Roberts (now Lord Clwyd). Years later, Sir Henry Cotton joined the Committe . Directly, and through the Indian Parliamentary Committee, the British Committee did, month by month and year by year, no end of work for India under the guidance of Sir William Wedderburn. The Committee conducted the journal *India*, first as a monthly and next as a weekly publication. Its first editor was the indefatigable and uncommonly well informed Mr. William Digby, and its most distinguished editor, Mr. Gordon Hewart, now Lord Hewart, Lord Chief Justice England.

Sir William Wedderburn

Sir William Wedderburn was the life and soul of all Indian work in England. An hereditary servant of India as he loved to call himself, Sir William Wedderburn uniformly acted in sympathy with Indians of all classes during the quarter of a century of his official life in Bombay as an I. C. S., while after retirement he dedicated to the service of this country every waking moment of the 29 years more given to him in this world.

He not only gave his time, he gave freely of his money. Religiously did he set apart the whole of his pension of £1,000 per annum derived from the Indian revenues for expenditure on Indian causes, and during the 29 years he lived after leaving India he must have spent several lakhs of rupees on and for us. He was in Parliament for seven years, and never was there a nobler member. After his presidentship of the Bombay Congress of 1889, he paid two visits to India—once in 1904 to attend the Bombay Congress presided over by Sir Henry Cotton and next in 1910 to preside over the Congress at Allahabad. Mr. Ranade told Mr. Gokhale that among all the Englishmen whom he had known there was none who could be compared to Sir William. Sir Surendranath Banerjea described him as "truly an Indian patriot in the garb of an English official" and added: "If Sir William Wedderburn's lot had been cast in more superstitious times, his contemporaries would have regarded him as the incarnation of some great Hindu Mahatma born again in the flesh for the well-being of his people." Mr. Gokhale knew him best and there was never any limit to his love and respect for him, while Sir William bore for him the love of a father for a son. Said Mr. Gokhale: "The picture of this great and venerable *rishi* of modern times is a picture that is too ennobling, too beautiful, too inspiring for words: it is a picture to dwell upon lovingly and reverentially and it is a picture to contemplate in silence." No words that I can employ will be worthy of being placed by the side of this beautiful tribute.

Leading Public men

A few words may be said of the leading political workers of the first twenty years of the Congress. Incomparably the greatest of them was one to whom a loving and reverential tribute has already been paid.

Dadabhai Naoroji

It was the unique distinction of Dadabhai Naoroji that he had created organized public life in India during forty years of tireless activity before the birth of the Congress and that he continued to be the one undisputed leader of Nationalist India for twenty-one years longer. (He lived ten years more in retirement.) I cannot commend too warmly to the younger generation of students of Indian politics Dadabhai Naoroji's monumental work *Poverty and un-British Rule in India*. They will see from it that he more than any other was the man who cleared the jungle, as it were, and laid out the broad tracks upon which public activities continued to run for long years if not until today. The drain of wealth from India was the central theme of Dadabhai Naoroji's innumerable discourses on Indian affairs. It was he more than any other who laid constant stress upon the manifold evils of political subjection. And there was no single important subject of which he did not make himself a master. For 61 long years, in England and in India, by day and by night, in circumstances favourable and adverse, in the face of discouragements which would have broken the heart of a smaller man, Dadabhai Naoroji served the Motherland with undeviating purpose, with complete selflessness and with vitality of faith, which would put to shame most younger men. For years he was the most moderate among public speakers, but in the latter part of his career continued disappointments drove him in spite of himself to employ language marked by great and increasing bitterness. Withal, he was the gentlest of souls and the most charitable in judgment, and never made a personal enemy. In respect equally of the highest personal character and the greatest public services Dadabhai Naoroji was the loftiest ideal his countrymen could set before themselves respectfully to follow at a distance.

Mahadeo Govind Ranade

Mahadeo Govind Ranade was second only to Dadabhai Naoroji. He bore spiritual kinship to him and the two had the greatest respect for each other. Ranade always spoke of the Grand Old Man as "Professor Dadabhai" because when Ranade was still a student Dadabhai Naoroji was already a professor, first in Elphinstone College, Bombay, and next in University College, London. If Dadabhai Naoroji was the greatest Indian patriot of the nineteenth century, Ranade was India's greatest thinker. While yet a student he gave promise of the rich career that was to follow. His answers to questions in the M.A. examination of Bombay University were so masterly that (it was said) Sir Alexander Grant sent them to the University of Edinburgh to serve as a model for students there. Ranade was mighty in intellect, a man of prodigious industry and of vast and various learning ; a profound thinker; an ardent patriot. Handicapped as he was by being in Government service all his life, he was a keen political worker, a religious reformer and a still more ardent social reformer, one of the greatest authorities on Indian economics, a great educationist, the inspirer and instructor of younger men who flocked to him. With all these rare accomplishments Ranade was the most modest, simple, courteous, unassuming of men, full of piety and the humility which is the invariable accompaniment of true greatness. Ranade's *Essays in Indian Economics*, *Essays in Religious and Social Reform* and *Rise of the Mahratta Power* should be read by every student and publicist of India.

Pherozeshah Mehta

Next there was Sir Pherozeshah Mehta. Majestic in appearance and stately in manners, Sir Pherozeshah Mehta was endowed with wonderful intellectual power. Having returned from England as a member of the bar in 1868, he put to immediate use the training in public life he had received from Dadabhai Naoroji in his student days and from that year (1868) onward until his death in 1915 he devoted the whole of those 47 years to brilliant service of the country. One instance may be given of his constructive political talent. Having entered the Bombay Corporation as early as 1868 he read three years later—at the early age of 26—a paper on Bombay municipal reform before the Bombay Branch of the East India Association. The constitution which he proposed then was substantially adopted by the Government and the Legislative Council, and in all essential respects is still the constitution of the premier municipal body of India. At sittings of the Indian National Congress, in the Bombay Legislative Council and in the Viceroy's Council, at conferences and public meetings, Sir Pherozeshah Mehta made contributions to Indian political thought unsurpassed not only in brilliant phrasing but in practical sagacity. Great as a speaker, he was the greatest debater that India has yet produced. And he was equalled by few in courage and independence. Fear was a quality unknown to him, and he was a born leader of men. The charm of his personality no one could resist. Dr. Rutherford, a Liberal member of Parliament who came to India in the winter of 1907, wrote in the *Manchester Guardian* that Sir Pherozeshah Mehta would be "the first man in the political kingdom in any country"; that in England he would have been Prime Minister but having been born in a subject country his life was condemned to barren criticism.

Gopal Krishna Gokhale

In the direct line of succession to Dadabhai Naoroji, Ranade and Sir Pherozeshah Mehta comes Mr. Gokhale. What he thought of Dadabhai Naoroji has already been stated. Ranade was his *guru* for twelve years. In Sir

Pherozeshah Mehta's judgment and motives he had such confidence that he used to say, "I would rather be wrong with Pherozeshah than right without him". Having led a life of poverty and hardship as a student, Mr. Gokhale, who possessed qualities which would have won him the richest prizes in life, while still in his teens voluntarily entered upon a life of privation and scarifice. Mr. Gokhale was an idealist all his life but a practical idealist. In his own words he set no limits to the aspirations of his countrymen, yet he had a constant and purposeful regard for what Mr. Spender has described as the "unceasing adjustments to changes of circumstances, thought and opinion (which) are of the essence of statesmanship". He recognized with Gladstone that not all questions were for all time and could distinguish between "impossible and realizable aims". It was Lord Morley's opinion that Mr. Gokhale unlike many others had "a politician's head and a sense of executive responsibility". In him there was complete harmony between thought, word and act and he was one of the very few men who never deviated from what he considered to be right, for any reason whatsoever. He emphatically condemned the immoral doctrine that the end justified the means. Rather did he believe that the prize was in the process. He was scrupulously conscientious in every transaction in life. Clear and powerful in intellect, hard-working to a fault, unsparing in exertion, Mr. Gokhale amassed knowledge at once vast, various and exact and was, like Lord Oxford and Asquith a master of direct expression and lucid exposition. He was so intellectually honest that he would never utter an opinion except after cross-examining himself severely and concluding that that opinion was sound and could not be shaken by criticism. Nor did he at any time show himself to be deficient in the complementary quality of intellectual courage which did not shrink from the conclusion to which the processes of thought led him, howsoever unpopular it might make him among a section of his countrymen, "more energetic than thoughtful" in his own language. He had a personality at once winning and forbidding, and in his presence younger men instinctively felt the distance that separated them from him and the impossibility of thinking a mean or selfish thought before him. Perhaps there were not many who were admitted to his intimacy, but the privileged few can never forget the combined charm and thoughtfulness of his observations in private talks on men and things. I used to feel as I sat listening to him that in the most casual way he was strewing roses before him. It is difficult to say whether his ability or his patriotism was greater. At the age of 31 he gave evidence in England before the Royal Commission on Indian Expenditure, which stamped him as a rare man. He was the greatest member of the Indian Legislative Council, and during the first four years of his membership carried on an almost singlehanded combat with so great a parliamentarian as Lord Curzon. Naturally the relations between the imperious imperialist and the fearless patriot were sometimes strained, but Lord Curzon had the greatest respect and admiration for him. "God has endowed you with extraordinary abilities" he once wrote to him, "and you have placed them unreservedly at the disposal of your country." To this day there is scarcely a public question in the consideration of which we do not get some light from a study of one or another of Mr. Gokhale's many great speeches. He made such impression upon British public men during successive visits to England that Mr. Massingham, the great editor of the *Nation*, remarked to me that there was no statesman in England comparable to Gokhale, that he was easily greater than Mr. Asquith himself. He added that Lord

Morley's success as Secretary of State for India was due chiefly to Mr. Gokhale's advice. To his very many services to the country Mr. Gokhale made a most valuable addition in 1905 when he established the Servants of India Society with an idea and ideal than which nothing could be loftier. That ideal is "devotion to Motherland so profound and so passionate that its very thought thrills and its actual touch lifts one out of oneself". I cite this from the great address delivered by Mr. Gokhale as President of the Congress at Benares six months after the foundation of the Servants of India Society. He was the youngest President of the Congress. He was only 39 then and yet one of the wisest and greatest of Presidents. It was a great speech which he made to Congress that year. But greater than the speech was the man. Mr. Gokhale, as I personally knew, could not sleep when any public matter caused him anxiety. It was nothing to him that his health was being ruined, he must at all times, in all conditions, think of the country and labour for the country. He has given me the motto "the patriot is the hero". He himself was the ideal patriot, and a hero to many of us.

If Ranade gave India Gokhale, Gokhale has given to India the Servants of India Society, which includes such men as Messrs. Srinivasa Sastri and Hirday Nath Kunzru. And it had until last week my friend Gopal Krishna Devadhar, the largest-hearted man I have known, a friend in need and deed in every case of distress. I mourn his death as a great loss to his countrymen. Mr. Gokhale wrote in the Preamble to the constitution of the Society :

A sufficient number of our countrymen must now come forward to devote themselves to the cause in the spirit in which religious work is undertaken. Public life must be spiritualized. Love of country must so fill the heart that all else shall appear as of little moment by its side. A fervent

6

patriotism which rejoices at every opportunity of sacrifice for the Motherland, a dauntless heart which refuses to be turned back from its object by difficulty or danger, a deep faith in the purpose of Providence which nothing can shake—equipped with these, the worker must start on his mission and reverently seek the joy which comes of spending oneself in the service of one's country.

Mr. Gokhale once said of Sir Bhashyam Iyengar that the very existence of such a man, who attained in his profession an eminence unequalled in his day or before or after him, was a service to the country as such men raised the stature of India before the world. My relation to Mr. Gokhale was that of a pupil to a master. Speaking with the respect that this relationship imposes, I will say that this very observation could be made of Mr. Gokhale himself. More than twenty years have elapsed since he left us. They have been years of trouble and difficulty, of strife and contention. During this period situations have arisen which called for the highest power of statesmanship from India's national leaders. We have had during this eventful period public men whose patriotism cannot be questioned, whose sacrifice and suffering for the Motherland must always evoke respect. But I venture to say that there has been no Gokhale since Gokhale. How often have not those of us whose inestimable privilege it was to be with Mr. Gokhale during the preceding ten or fifteen years have not had occasion to cry in sheer despair, "Oh for an hour of Gokhale!"

Dinshaw Eduljee Wacha

It is impossible to leave the Bombay presidency without giving a respectful thought to Sir Dinshaw Wacha. One of the trinity of Parsi political leaders, Sir Dinshaw Wacha is among those patriots who have never spared themselves in the service of the country. A journalist who wrote here, there and everywhere; a private correspondent the most regular, voluminous and outspoken; secretary of the Bombay Presidency Association and of the Indian National Congress ; a member of public bodies too numerous to mention but active in every one of them ; always helpful and generous to younger public men ; one of the most careful and assiduous students of problems of economics, finance and statistics, Dinshaw Eduljee Wacha was for nearly two generations one of the most constant and relentless critics of policy and measures and his speeches and writings constitute a mine of information in which students of Indian politics can profitably delve. Now in his 92nd year and living in retirement, I am glad to say that he is still in good health and what is more remarkable, he continues to be a devoted student of affairs.[1] He told me when I saw him a couple of years ago that he had not missed a single number of the *Economist* since the year 1861 ! He was one of those who used to consider it a religious duty not to miss a solitary session of the Congress. He presided over the session held at Calcutta in 1901. Vast was the contribution he made to Indian political development during the many years of his active life.

Other Leaders

Other eminent men of the western presidency during this period whose names are deserving of mention as distinguished public workers include Badruddin Tyabji, Kashinath Trimbak Telang, Bal Gangadhar Tilak, Rahimatulla Muhammad Sayani (who presided over the Congress in 1896), Jhaverilal Umiashankar Yajnik, Narayan Ganesh Chandavarkar, Gokuldas Kahandas Parekh, Hormusji Ardesher Wadya, K. N. Bahadurji, Bhalchandra Krishna, Daji Abaji Khare, Chimanlal Harilal Setalvad, Raghunath Pandurang Karandikar, Narayan Vishnu Gokhale, Narayan Madhav Samarth, Ambalal Sakerlal Desai and Hari Sitaram Dikshit. Mr. Tyabji, a

---

[1]Sir Dinshaw has since passed away.

great advocate and great orator, was the first Muslim leader who identified himself with the Congress. After his elevation to the bench of the High Court in 1895 he used, as Sir Pherozeshah Mehta once said, to create occasions publicly to declare—and from the bench, too !—that he was still a Congressman.—Kashinath Trimbak Telang was scholar, educationist, lawyer and politician. A great orator and an equally great debater, Telang was a profound scholar and possessed a luminous intellect. After an academic career of a brilliance scarcely equalled and never surpassed, which yet was completed by the age of 19, Telang rose rapidly to the position of a leader of the bar and distinctions were showered upon him in rapid and unceasing succession. He was appointed a member of the Indian Education Commission when he was only 32 and a member of the Bombay Legislative Council three years later. He became a judge of the High Court at the age of 39 and vice-chancellor of the University two years later. Alas, he died at the very early age of 43. Of what mental mould he was made I would ask you to judge for yourselves by a study of Mr. Ranade's illuminating discourse entitled *The Telang School of Thought**.—Mr. Sayani, the second Muslim President of the Congress, made in his address a statement on the position of Muslims in India, which I regard as the most comprehensive, instructive and impartial treatment of the subject made by any one to this day.—Mr. Yajnik was equally informed and thoughtful, and the volume of his essays published in 1902 will be instructive reading even today.—Sir Gokuldas Parekh did such work on the land revenue question during and after the famine of 1900 that his criticisms eventually compelled the Government of Bombay

---

*Delivered at the Hindu Union Club, Bombay, in 1898 and included in the volume of Ranade's "Essays in Religious and Social Reform".

to change their policy. The Government of Bombay, taking advantage of the necessitous condition of the ryots due to that famine, passed in 1901 in the teeth of bitter opposition an amendment to the Land Revenue Code, on account of which there was the first organized walk-out from the Council as a demonstration of protest, and the leader was Sir Pherozeshah Mehta. The other four members who followed him were Messrs. Gokhale and Khare, and Sir Gokuldas Parekh and Sir Bhalchandra Krishna.—Sir Narayan Chandavarkar went as a delegate to England in 1885 with Messrs. Manomohan Ghose and Salem Ramaswami Mudaliar, acted as one of the secretaries of the Presidency Association for several years and presided over the Congress in the year 1900.—Dr. Bahadurji, who joined the Congress in 1893, brought to the fore the necessity of reorganization of the medical services of India. His advocacy of this reform was marked by uncommon ability and zeal. He succeeded in bringing the question into such prominence that he was called upon in 1896 to give evidence before the Royal Commission on Indian Expenditure commonly called the Welby Commission. His early death in 1898 when he was still in his thirties, was a great loss to public life. The reform which he advocated continues to be a pressing topic of the day. If instead of redressing our grievance the Government have actually taken some backward steps such as the substitution of nomination for competition in the recruitment of the Indian Medical Service the cause is the same as in other matters, *viz.*, that India has no national government. —Mr. Tilak's political career deserves and requires fuller treatment. I reserve it for the next section as I think it will be more appropriately included in the period that follows.

Surendranath Banerjea

Of public men in Bengal during this period as well as in the following, indubitably the leading figure was Surendranath Banerjea. One of the very few Indians who could join the Indian Civil Service in the sixties of the last century, he had the misfortune of being dismissed after a few years for a technical error. Thereby the loss of the Government became the gain of the country. He chose education and journalism as his vocations and actively took to public life. He was first befriended by Iswar Chandra Vidyasagar and appointed a professor in his college, then called the Metropolitan Institution and now known as Vidyasagar College. Surendranath Banerjea later founded Ripon College, where he was professor of English for many years. As previously mentioned, he took over the *Bengalee* from Mr. W. C. Bonnerjee, edited it as a weekly for 17 years, and then expanded it into a daily. He founded in collaboration with Mr. Ananda Mohan Bose the Indian Association which, as I have said, is still flourishing (as a Liberal institution). He joined the Indian National Congress at its second session held at Calcutta in 1886 and immediately became one of its acknowledged leaders. Whoever might be the president Surendranath Banerjea was, session after session, the central figure in the Congress. He was a great orator. Second only to Mr. Lalmohan Ghose in what Sir Pherozeshah Mehta described as "rare and unrivalled powers of oratory", Surendranath Banerjea excelled him in the power of mass appeal. Sir Henry Cotton wrote of him in his book *New India*, that from Multan to Chittagong Surendranath Banerjea could by the power of his tongue raise a revolt or suppress a rebellion. He twice presided over the Congress and on both occasions performed a marvellous feat of memory by delivering very long addresses correct to a word, but without reference to the printed copy. He visited England four times on India's business and every time his oratory won great admiration from the most competent judges. I was a witness of how by one speech he converted opponents into supporters of Mr. Montagu's India Bill of 1919. For years he was the most distinguished member of the Bengal Legislative Council and later became a member of the Indian Legislative Council. In his autobiography entitled *A Nation in Making*, published shortly before his death, he gave an account of fifty years of public life. It shows that he is entitled to be remembered as one of the makers of modern Bengal. He was one of the first ministers under Mr. Montagu's Act and justified himself in that capacity by restoring to the Calcutta municipality the right of self-government of which it had been deprived in 1899. Surendranath Banerjea is one of the names which can never be ignored in any account of the political and national progress of India.

Other Bengal Leaders

Of other eminent Bengali politicians of this period the first place should be given to Mr. W. C. Bonnerjee, twice president of the Congress and one of the greatest leaders of the Calcutta bar—a man distinguished by uncommon power of judgment. Next there was Mr. Manmohan Ghose, whose work on the question of separation of judicial from executive functions cannot be forgotten. Mr. Romesh Chandra Dutt came into public life in 1898 after retirement from the Indian Civil Service and presided over the Congress at Lucknow in 1899. Mr. Dutt's works, *India under Early British Rule*, *India in the Victorian Age* and *Famines and Land Assessments in India* may be warmly commended to students of Indian politics.

A. M. Bose

Ananda Mohan Bose was second only to Surendranath Banerjea as an earnest worker. Most graceful of orators, the founder of City College, one of the founders of the Sadharana Brahma Samaj, and equally keen as social and temperance reformer, Anandá Mohan Bose was thought of so highly by Lord Ripon that he was invited hy him to be the president of the Indian Education Commission of 1882, when he was only 35 years old. But Mr. Bose argued that the report of a commission under an Indian president would not carry the same weight with the Government as one presided over by a senior British official, and therefore only accepted a membership. In the power of intellect Mr. A. M. Bose was the equal of any of his contemporaries and would have attained a position of pre-eminence in any line of activity to which he might have chosen to apply himself with concentration. But his patriotism was so great that, in the language of his brother-in-law, Sir J. C. Bose, he "broke his genius into fragments" in order to serve the country in every sphere of national life. His later years were clouded by persistent illness. His last public appearance was pathetic. Unable to move but equally unable to stay at home, he was carried in a chair to a great popular demonstration on the day the partition of Bengal was effectuated and there delivered the most feeling of speeches.—Another leader of the front rank was Babu Kali Churn Banurji, Christian by religion but nationalist in every fibre of his being. He too was a great orator, and he was most devoted to the Congress. It was an accident that he did not preside over it. His qualities cannot be better summed up than they were by Sir Rashbehary Ghosh when he said : "We cannot help feeling how much learning, how much modest and unassuming simplicity, how much piety, how much winsome tenderness and how much patriotism lie buried in the grave of Kali Churn Banurji."

G. Subramania Iyer

In Madras the principal public worker was Mr. G. Subramania Iyer. He did for Madras, principally through the columns of the *Hindu* but also through the Congress and the Mahajana Sabha, what men like Surendranath Banerjea and Motilal Ghosh did for Bengal and Wacha, Tilak and Gokhale for Bombay. He was the greatest Indian journalist of his generation and the greatest admirer of his writings was Mr. Hume. Mr. Hume wrote to Mr. Subramania Iyer that his articles would do credit even to the *Times* of London, and he selected the *Hindu*, of which he purchased fifty copies, as the best medium of instruction of sympathetic members of Parliament. Pherozeshah Mehta and Dinshaw Wacha equally admired him, while Mr. Gokhale told me one day that there was no other editor in India who had the same masterly grip of public questions as Mr. Subramania Iyer. He was among the Indian witnesses before the Royal Commission on Indian Expenditure. He was also a practical social reformer. He was not but deserved to be president of the Congress. Mr. Subramania Iyer wrote a very useful book entitled *Some Economic Aspects of British Rule in India*.

Other public men of Madras who should be named include Sir S. Subramania Iyer, noted for wisdom and charity ; Mr. Ananda Charlu, unfailing in independence ; Sir Sankaran Nair, who delivered one of the best of Congress presidential addresses in a year of the greatest difficulty ; Messrs. C. Vijiaraghavachariar distinguished for fearlessness and N. Subbarau Pantulu, able, shrewd and wise ; Mr. M. Viraraghavachariar of the *Hindu* ; Diwan Bahadur P. Kesava Pillai of Gooty ; Mr. P. Rangiah Naidu, for many years the president of the Mahajana Sabha and chairman of the reception committee of the Congress of 1894 ; Messrs.

S. A. Swaminatha Iyer of Tanjore and G. Venkataratnam and K. Perraju of Cocanada.

V. Krishnaswami Iyer

In the later years of this period came into prominence the most brilliant man that I have known in the Madras presidency and one of the most brilliant in the country, my most kind friend, Mr. V. Krishnaswami Iyer. Equal to Lord Oxford and Asquith in quickness of apprehension and to Lord Haldane in elasticity of brain, very vigorous and still more frank in speech, effective in debate, Mr. Krishnaswami Iyer was equally distinguished by judgment, courage, public spirit and philanthropy. If Pherozeshah Mehta, Ajodhia Nath and Lajpat Rai were the lions of Bombay, the United Provincess and the Punjab, respectively, Krishnaswami Iyer if anybody was the lion of Madras. "Krishnaswami Iyer's brain works at least twice as quickly as mine and it is not easy for me to keep pace with him," remarked Mr. Gokhale when he had to act with him in a sub-committee. "It will be many years" said Mr. Govindaraghava Iyar on the day of Mr. Krishnaswami Iyer's death, "before we can find one who can anything like adequately fill his place, at any rate in our part of the country." Nearly 24 years have passed since that melancholy event and I think it true to say that the void has not yet been filled.

Pandit Ajodhia Nath

In the United Provinces Pandit Ajodhia Nath, as stated earlier, died a premature death after a public life all too brief but highly distinguished. He had no equal in fearlessness and he had a forceful personality. He was a born leader. Fortunately he left to us in his son, my friend and colleague Pandit Hirday Nath Kunzru, a son of whom Mr. Gokhale, his master, predicted, "Now Hirday Nath is known as Pandit Ajodhia Nath's son, a day will come when Pandit

Ajodhia Nath will be known as Hirday Nath's father". Who that has followed Mr. Kunzru's splendid public career can have a doubt that Mr. Gokhale's prediction has already been realized ?—After Pandit Ajodhia Nath there was Pandit Bishambhar Nath, who joined the Congress earlier than his more brilliant junior and who remained faithful to the creed to the day of his death in 1907 at the ripe age of 76.—Then there were Pandit Bishan Narayan Dar and Babu Ganga Prasad Varma of Lucknow. Bishan Narayan Dar was one of the most learned yet most modest of men and he was so great as a writer that many of his writings still live. If he had been in better health and had been less modest the country would have known more of him.—Ganga Prasad Varma was essentially a remarkable example of a self-made man who by sheer moral qualities made himself one of the most conspicuous figures in public life. No one knew him without respecting him. His death in 1914 at the early age of 51 inflicted upon his city and province a blow from which they have not yet fully recovered. It is true to say that he has left no successor behind at Lucknow.

Pandit Madan Mohan Malaviya

The principal public man of the United Provinces was then and is now Pandit Madan Mohan Malaviya. He presents to us the rare spectacle of a man who was recognized as a leader almost from the very start of his career. Of either the personal qualities or the public services of this extraordinary man it is difficult to speak in a few words. He was a favourite of Mr. Hume's. It was he who, in conjunction with Babu Ganga Prasad Varma, kept the Congress flag flying in the United Provinces in all those years. Profoundly religious, he has lived a life of piety, goodness, simplicity and unselfishness. Never blessed with robust health, he yet has never known what it is to take rest from work, and all his work is public work.

About to complete the age of 74 and in very feeble health, he is still as active as he has always been since he entered public life 53 years ago. Twice president of the Congress, today he is still in the Congress though it may be doubted if he is of the Congress. He has given the country among several other institutions the Benares Hindu University, the greatest of them all. It is an imperishable monument to the greatness of Malaviyaji's life.

British friends

Among British friends of India of that period special mention should be made, after Mr. Hume and Sir William Wedderburn, of Messrs. W. S. Caine and William Digby. The former served India in Parliament, in the British Committee of the Congress and the Indian Parliamentary Committee, and specially through an organization founded by himself, the Anglo-Indian Temperance Association, of which another genuine friend of India, Mr. Samuel Smith, was the President. Mr. Samuel Smith came to India to preside over the All India Temperance Conference at Calcutta in 1906, but died in sleep the night before. Mr. Digby was one of the very few British journalists out in India who completely identified themselves with the people of the country. He did valuable work in England for many years. His outstanding service was his great book *'Prosperous' British India,* which should be read with its companion volume, Dadabhai Naoroji's *Poverty and un-British Rule,* to enable one to form an adequate idea of the grinding poverty of India and of the grave economic injury of alien rule.

The Press

The press made great progress during the first 20 years of the Congress. The *Hindu,* the *Amrita Bazar Patrika* and the *Bengalee* became daily newspapers, while newspapers in Indian languages increased in number, in circulation and in public usefulness. During this period

Mr. G. Parameswaran Pillai took over the *Madras Standard* and edited it with brilliant ability during the few years that were vouchsafed to him. Mr. Parameswaran Pillai was an ardent Congressman. Mr. G. Subramania Iyer started in 1903 an English weekly paper, *United India*, which was remarkably good, and he edited the *Swadesamitran*, the Tamil paper which he took over after leaving the *Hindu*. Mr. N. N. Ghose's *Indian Nation* and Mr. Malabari's *Indian Spectator*, published at Calcutta and Bombay respectively, were the most thoughtful of weekly papers in the whole country. The *Indian Union* was issued from Allahabad, first with Pandit Madan Mohan Malaviya and next my friend Babu Brahmananda Sinha as editor, but it did not last more than a few years. The chief paper in the United Provinces throughout this period was Babu Ganga Prasad Varma's *Advocate* (Lucknow), in which Pandit Bishan Narayan Dar wrote some of his brilliant articles. Its efforts were supplemented in the last three years of this period by the *Indian People*, started at Allahabad in 1903 by Mr. Sachchidananda Sinha but since incorporated with the *Leader*. In the Punjab the *Tribune* established itself as one of the best papers in the country with Mr. N. Gupta as its editor. When Sir Dennis FitzPatrick was Lieutenant-Governor of the Punjab, the *Tribune* was almost a power in the province; so much so, that the local (Lahore) Anglo-Indian paper, the *Civil and Military Gazette* once inquired whether the province was being governed by Sir Dennis or by the *Tribune*.

CHAPTER III

(1905-1919)

PARTITION OF BENGAL AND AFTER

The partition of Bengal

The political situation as it developed in the following decade and a half had its beginnings a few years earlier. It was for the first time in 1903 that the voice of the extremist in Indian politics attracted attention. Babu Bipin Chandra Pal, who had joined the Congress in 1887 at Madras, began to write in a weekly paper which he was then editing (*New India*), in terms of disapproval of the method of political agitation which was the only one in vogue. The then Maharaja of Natore, who had been chairman of the reception committee of the Congress at Calcutta in 1901, was the first person to characterize constitutional agitation as "political mendicancy". Pursuing the same vein of thought Mr. A. Chaudhuri (afterwards Justice Sir Asutosh Chaudhuri), who always had a weakness for epigrammatic expression, said in one sentence in his presidential address to the Bengal Provincial Conference at Burdwan in 1904, "A subject race has no politics". The provoking cause of these expressions of impatience was the policy of Lord Curzon, which nearly exasperated public opinion, specially in Bengal. By that time the project of the partition of Bengal was already in the air. When it was carried into effect in the following year, in a form still more unacceptable to the Bengali race than the first proposals, the people of that province nearly grew mad with rage. As if the partition by itself were not enough, the first Lieutenant-Governor of Eastern Bengal, Sir Bampfylde Fuller, openly announced a policy of preference for Muslims and prejudice against Hindus and deliberately embarked upon a campaign of repression and humiliation of the Hindus. The people of Bengal employed the method of the boycott of British goods as the most effective means of drawing pointed attention in England to their greatest grievance. This was the signal for a division of opinion in Congress ranks, which later became increasingly acute. Inside the Congress the first echoes of this were heard at the Benares session. The first act of the extremists was to oppose in the subjects committee a resolution of welcome to their Royal Highnesses the Prince and Princess of Wales—our present King-Emperor[1] and Queen-Empress—who were then on a visit to India. In the recently published volume of the letters of Lord Minto there is a passage which makes out that Mr. Gokhale was a leading promoter of the idea of boycott of the royal visitors. I suppose this is how history is written! Of course Mr. Gokhale had nothing to do with any manner of opposition to or abstention from a cordial and respectful welcome to their Royal Highnesses. He was not made that way. In the subjects committee of the Congress the lead in opposition was taken by Mr. Tilak and Lala Lajpat Rai, and those who discouraged, resisted and defeated their effort were led by Mr. Gokhale, Mr. R. C. Dutt and Mr. Surendranath Banerjea. The principal topic of contention at that Congress was the question of boycott. In the end a wise compromise was reached and members of both ways of thinking could support it with equal strength. Agitation as well as repression grew in volume and intensity. The annual session of the Bengal Provincial Conference, held at Barisal under a Muslim president, Mr. A. Rasul, was dispersed by the police under orders of the Lieutenant-Governor, Sir Bampfylde Fuller. He resigned a few

[1] His Majesty King George V passed away in January, 1936.

weeks later owing to an order of the Secretary of State, Mr. John Morley, of which he disapproved. The division of opinion between the two sections grew steadily apace, and the situation so developed by the autumn of 1906 that it became clear that a successful session of the Congress would only be possible that year if Dadabhai Naoroji, then in England and 81 years of age, could be persuaded to come out as President. It was a great Congress that assembled in Calcutta under his illustrious presidency, but in committee it was also easily the most uproarious and almost rebellious session that I witnessed. The discourtesy with which all the older leaders were greeted was painful. Intolerance was the order of the day and the most honoured of veterans either managed to get a hearing by sheer persistence, or failed to get any. Again salvation was sought in compromise, which was only rendered possible by the presence in the chair of the Grand Old Man. The compromise saved that session from breaking up but proved unhappy in the sequel as it was interpreted in a different way by either section and an embittered campaign against the older leaders was kept up throughout the following year, chiefly under the leadership of Mr. Tilak.

1907

The year 1907 brought in its train nothing but trouble to the country. The Punjab was the storm-centre. The policy of the Lieutenant-Governor, Sir Denzil Ibbetson, was reactionary and his measures were provocative. Among other measures the Colonization Bill produced acute discontent. The agitation was met on the part of the Government by the deportation of Lala Lajpat Rai and another, under Bengal Regulation III of 1818, by the wholesale prosecution of respected men in Rawalpindi and by a Seditious Meetings Ordinance. This was later made an Act of the legislature. Quiet was only restored when the Colonization Bill was vetoed by Lord Minto. In Bengal the agitation against the partition was kept up in full vigour. Press prosecutions followed by severe sentences were the order of the day. Extremist agitation under Mr. Tilak's leadership increased in volume and bitterness and extended to the whole country. East Bengal was disgraced by the worst communal riots, in which Sir Bampfylde Fuller's policy of preference for Muslims was followed by his successor and by the officials of the province. This policy was carried to such lengths that actually " a sessions judge divided witnesses into two classes, Hindus and Muhammadans, and preferred the evidence of Muhammadans to Hindus because they are Muhammadans". At one place, "some Muslims proclaimed by beat of drum that the Government had permitted them to loot the Hindus", while at another they publicly declared, according to a magistrate, " that the Government had permitted the Muhammadans to marry Hindu widows in the *nika* form". One savage outbreak followed the wide circulation, among the Muhammadans in East Bengal, of a " red pamphlet " the contents of which are so abominable that I think I had better not say more about it. By the end of the year quiet was restored in the Punjab, Lala Lajpat Rai himself having been set free after six months, but Bengal continued to be in a disturbed condition. The whole country was in a state of ferment. The Congress was to be held at Nagpur, but the meeting of the reception committee at which the president was to be elected broke up in disorder. The venue was changed to Surat, where Congressmen made preparations on a large scale at very short notice, but the Congress was not destined to be held. It assembled only to break up amidst scenes of violence before the President proceeded even with the opening paragraph of his address. The feelings between the two parties were extremely embittered and opinion in the country was acutely divided.

The old party met in convention on the ruins of the Congress and set up a committee which, meeting at Allahabad four months later, drew up a constitution for the Congress. The first article of the Constitution declared :

Swaraj

> The objects of the Indian National Congress are the attainment by the people of India of a system of government similar to that enjoyed by self-governing members of the British empire and a participation by them in the rights and responsibilities of the empire on equal terms with those members. These objects are to be achieved by constitutional means by bringing about a steady reform of the existing system of administration and by promoting national unity, fostering public spirit and developing and organizing the intellectual, moral, economic and industrial resources of the country.

The word "Swaraj" was, if I mistake not, first used by Mr. Tilak sometime in the nineties of the last century but it did not catch ; just as the Swadeshi movement, as it is understood today, was also advocated about that very time by Mr. Tilak himself but it too found no echo in the public mind. It was Mr. Gokhale who first read a paper before a London Association on self-government for India. In the Congress of 1904 the President, Sir Henry Cotton, who had lately retired from service after having been cheated of the position of Lieutenant-Governor of Bengal due to Lord Curzon's dissatisfaction with him for his advocacy of the cause of the coolies against the planters in Assam, enunciated the ideal of the Indian patriot as "the establishment of a federation of free and separate states, the united states of India, placed on a fraternal footing with the self-governing colonies, each with its own local autonomy, cemented together under the ægis of Great Britain". In the following year the President, Mr. Gokhale, said that the goal of the Congress was "that in course of time a form of government should be attained in this country similar to what exists in the self-governing colonies of the British empire". At the Congress of 1906 the

President, Dadabhai Naoroji, definitely held up "self-government or Swaraj, like that of the United Kingdom or the colonies, as the ideal of the Congress". It was an address which was described by Mr. Surendranath Banerjea as "the political scripture of India". What had until then been only said in speeches was declared formally and authoritatively as the goal of the Congress in the Constitution of 1908.

Old and new parties

The first Congress under the new constitution was held at Madras, thanks to the determination of Mr. Krishnaswami Iyer. It followed its even tenor in subsequent years until 1915 when Lord (then Sir S. P.) Sinha presided and declared as our ideal the idea embodied in Abraham Lincoln's historic phrase, "government of the people for the people by the people". Throughout these years the controversy between the old and the new party was kept up, sometimes raging furiously, at other times less violently, but always alive. The new party did not care to join the Congress. They illustrated then by their continued abstention what the Liberals have since done, namely, that the Congress is a propagandist organization in which there is no room for more parties than one. They then acted on the footing, as the Liberals have done in later years, that there is no analogy between a propagandist organization and a legislature, and while every shade of opinion must be represented in the latter which makes laws which affect all the people and imposes taxes payable by all, the Congress as a propagandist organization exists to advocate particular opinions and it is crippled in its effort if there are in it parties speaking in different voices. During some of those years Congress sessions evoked less enthusiasm than when it had been an united body. But as year succeeded year increasing numbers flocked to its standard.

All the same it has to be recognized that popular sentiment was more strongly in favour of the more radical politicians. The latter included more of the younger men, full of energy, enthusiasm and zeal. They were able to make a more popular appeal than the older party. Briefly put, they told the people : "You have grievances. You get no redress. You are impoverished. Many of you are starving. The educated men have no adequate scope for their talents. The people are humiliated and treated by men in authority as inferior beings. Why, because the Government is foreign. What is the remedy ? To replace it by our own." The older constitutional leaders, however, had of necessity to put in qualifications and make explanations as to why they did not urge heroic courses of action. Honestly, they had to speak not only of the evils of foreign rule but also of the limitations of our countrymen. Mr. Gokhale used to put it in this way. Foreign rule is certainly evil, but why was it rendered possible ? Could any foreigners have established themselves in India if there had not been something seriously wrong with the people of the country ? Is it not an historical fact that the evil of foreign rule was only rendered possible by antecedent evils in the body politic ? Have we been able to remove them ? Is it not necessary to remove them and to make ourselves fit before we could hope either to achieve or to retain Swaraj ? It is a commonplace of mass psychology that a complicated argument cannot be intelligently followed by the man in the street, that a simple categorical statement is more easily appreciated, that a simpler and loftier ideal attracts the heart more than one which requires explanation, and also, that impassioned appeals to passion, prejudice and vanity are more effective as propaganda than the calm, cool, informed and learned arguments of moderate leaders. Yet another difficulty of the latter has always been that they cannot hold meetings and get a hearing because of the antics of some of the extremer men who have made intolerance their very own. The present-day Liberals have lost the freedom of speech at public meetings far more by the attitude of Congress zealots than by any legislative or administrative act of the Government. The extremists can easily please their countrymen while more moderate men are driven to a choice between serving the country and pleasing the more vociferous of their countrymen. Yet one more difficulty has always to be faced by the latter. The Government is so little responsive to appeals to its sense of reason and justice that they are not able to point to a record of achievement by which to impress their countrymen. The differences between the two sections are temperamental. They are not differences on particular questions. They are differences of outlook and of method which cut diagonally across the whole field of public life. No wonder then that in those years as in these still more than then, the extremer the gospellor the more does he command the ear of the multitude.

More repression

In the country as a whole agitation was kept up almost at white heat. The partition of Bengal, "a settled fact" (Lord Morley) but "an unsettled question" (Sir Rashbehary Ghosh), continued to be a festering sore in the body politic. Repression of open political activities drove agitation underground. Sir Edward Baker, Lieutenant-Governor of Bengal, boasted that he was not afraid of this and everything would be all right if the preaching of sedition was stopped. The terrorist activities of all the years that have followed have tragically proved the blunder of this short-sighted view. Prosecutions of writers and speakers continued to be the order of the day. In the middle of 1908 Mr. Tilak was again prosecuted for sedition and sentenced to transportation for six years. Almost no other leader of the party was saved. The first bomb outrage was perpetrated at Muzaffarpur on April 30, 1908, when an attempt to kill Mr. Kingsford, who as chief presidency magistrate of Calcutta had sent to jail many a person accused of political offences, actually led by mistaken identity to the murder of Mrs. and Miss Kennedy, wife and daughter of Mr. Pringle Kennedy, who had been an active Congressman in earlier years. The Government met this by two pieces of legislation, the Explosive Substances Act and the Incitement to Offences Act. A conspiracy was unearthed in Calcutta and a host of persons were accused of participation in it. The principal one among them was Mr. Aravindo Ghosh, who had come into politics a couple of years earlier.

Mr. Aravindo Ghose

Having been rejected for the I.C.S., Mr. Aravindo Ghose served in Baroda as a teacher before returning home to Calcutta and taking to political life. He edited a paper in English, the *Bande Mataram*. His command of English is wonderful and his writings in a quasi-metaphysical vein and in rich literary garb, and always fiery in their political outlook, were enjoyed and admired by the readers day by day, but they were calculated to inflame the popular mind. Mr. Aravindo Ghosh was fortunately acquitted of the heinous offence with which he was charged. It was then that as his counsel a man who in later years was destined to play a dominant part in public life, first became an all-India figure. I refer to Mr. C.R. Das. Mr. Aravindo Ghosh soon after retired from politics and British India and has found his proper place as a profound exponent of subjects religious and philosophical. He has enriched India's literature by contributions to these subjects which I venture to think will live.

Deportations

In the last month of that year—1908—several public men of Bengal including Babus Aswini Kumar Dutt and Krishna Kumar Mitra were deported under Regulation III of 1818, a "lawless law" as Sir Rashbehary Ghosh described it. In the same month the Criminal Law Amendment Act was passed, part II of which has since been used most extensively for declaring associations unlawful. In a word, it may be said that Government tried hard to meet agitation not by redress of grievances but by repression. This has been the age-old vice of irresponsible governments and we in India have only too much reason to remember this all our lives, as the history of all the years that have followed and down to this day testifies.

Reform

But was repression the only policy of Government ? No, it must be mentioned to the credit of Lord Morley and Lord Minto, the Secretary of State and the Viceroy, respectively, during these years that they early felt convinced of the necessity of political reform. The Act of 1892 had clearly outgrown its utility and the Councils established under it must be replaced by legislatures which would give a little more satisfaction to the people. Curiously enough, the first fruit of this zeal for reform found expression in a scheme published on August 23. 1907, over the signature of Sir Harold Stuart, then home secretary in the Government of India. A scheme of 'reform' ! This description of it was grotesque. It was more of a practical joke. It embodied proposals so reactionary, so objectionable, so harmful to the country that no good word for it was said by any man worthy of mention anywhere in India. That scheme was based, avowedly, on the theory that a "counterpoise" to the influence of educated Indians must be found and this was sought in a so-called "council of notables" and in class and communal representation carried to excess. The Madras Government's proposals made a *reductio ad absurdum* of this scheme. They proposed separate representation for castes and for occupations. Their proposals were simply laughed out of court. By far the best criticism of this scheme was made by Pandit Bishan Narayan Dar at the United Provinces Conference at Lucknow in 1908. Thanks to the presence of John Morley at the India Office and to the great work done by Mr. Gokhale as India's spokesman before him the scheme of 1907 was rejected and in its place came the Dispatch of the Secretary of State dated December 17, 1908. The Indian Councils Act of 1909 was based upon it. On the whole, Lord Morley's substituted scheme was favourably received in India. The numerical strength of the Councils was increased, the right of interpellation was extended and members were allowed to move resolutions on the budget. Nonofficial majorities were conceded in the provinces. Two years earlier two Indians were appointed for the first time to the Secretary of State's Council, and concurrently with the reform of the Legislative Councils one Indian member was appointed to the Executive Councils of the Viceroy and the Governors of Madras and Bombay. An Executive Council was established in Bengal with an Indian member. The proposal to establish a similar council in the United Provinces was defeated by a vote of the House of Lords. It was again in 1915. It is due to Lord Minto that we should acknowledge the support which he gave to these reforms, while Lord Morley deserves credit for having succeeded in putting them through, notwithstanding great difficulties he encountered, specially in respect of the appointment of an Indian to the Governor-General's Executive Council. It is amusing to recall that the leader of the Opposition in the House of Lords, Lord Lansdowne, a former Viceroy of India, complained bitterly that a "foreign element" was being introduced into the Government of India, the "foreign" in India being the Indian ! As in the case of the Act of 1892, so in the case of the Act of 1919 much of the good that the Act itself might have done was undone by the nature of the rules made thereunder. Here is another illustration of the unequalled capacity of the bureaucracy to defeat reform in detail.

Communal electorates

There is no rose without a thorn. The Act of 1909 brought with it an evil which has since been aggravated. It is the evil of separate communal electorates. Lord Minto was its author. He received at Simla on October 1, 1906, an influential deputation representative of Muslims of the whole country, led by his Highness the Aga Khan. The deputation made preposterous claims and frankly preached the gospel of separatism. Lord Minto at once committed himself and the Government to the most unreasonable and unwise of demands in the most thoughtless manner and with almost suspicious completeness. It is now a matter of common knowledge that the deputation was not altogether spontaneous. The inspiration came from Simla. Evidently the more clever of the officials of the Home department thought to counter the reforms which they knew were certain to come, by driving a wedge between the two great communities of the land. They evidently thought to themselves what some more free and less responsible, because unofficial, Englishmen in India did not hesitate to say openly, "If Hindus and Muslims united, where should we be ?" Here again Lord Morley in his dispatch of 1908 tried to minimize the evil by proposing joint electorates with reservation of seats, but an agitation against these proposals was immediately engineered in India. The Government of India were hostile to Lord Morley's proposal and they would not be defeated. They had in the Home department at the time a very resourceful and equally reactionary official, Sir Herbert Risley, and there were among Muslims men who did not hesitate to seek what they thought was an advantage to their community by organizing a communal agitation which exactly suited the purposes of the official opponents of Lord Morley's proposal.[1] The agitation was carried to England, where the leaders were the Aga Khan and the late Mr. Ameer Ali. It found spokesmen in the House of Commons, most prominent among them being the present Marquess of Zetland, Secretary of State for India, then Earl of Ronaldshay, afterwards Governor of Bengal, and the late Sir William Joynson-Hicks, afterwards Viscount Brentford. The agitation succeeded. Lord Morley yielded, perhaps he had to yield if his Bill was not to be wrecked in Parliament. Since then separate electorates have been extended in some provinces to local bodies and everywhere to other communities. Even women, who all but unanimously protested that they did not want to be dragged into the vortex of communal electorates and communal strife, have been dragooned into them under the Act passed this year. The experience of communal electorates gained during the last quarter of a century enables one to give a clear verdict against them. To convert the legislature into a museum of representatives of a dozen or more separate communities and interests is to divide its members into persons owning so many separate allegiances and to prevent them from being loyal to the one supreme entity, The People. Elected majorities have proved on the majority of occasions to be futile due to the division of members into representatives of separate communal and sectional electorates. I anticipate that our experience in future legislatures will not be more agreeable.

1. A Muslim leader has since declared that it is the right of minorities to be treacherous to the country !

The Press Act

I must come back for a minute to repression. It is an irony of fate that almost the first legislative measure of the first Morley-Minto Council should have been the Press Act of 1910. This Act was passed in great hurry on the plea that terrorist activities were being encouraged by scurrilous writings in the press. The Press Bill in its original form was, I learnt on reliable authority, far more draconian. But the Indian Law Member refused to be a party to it and tendered his resignation when he found himself in a minority in the Executive Council. Neither Lord Morley nor Lord Minto was willing to lose Mr. (S. P.) Sinha. The result was a compromise measure. Some of the I. C. S. men in the Government of India never forgave him for his part in that affair. He, however, was still dissatisfied with the result and proposed to abstain from voting on it in the Council, but he was advised not to go to that length as the Secretary of State and the Viceroy had for his sake made the Bill a little less objectionable. Lord Sinha's position was so misunderstood in the country, he was subjected to such attacks for years, that when the last of them by Mr. Eardley Norton was published in 1919, I made public in the columns of a newspaper in England the correct facts as they had been told me by Mr. Gokhale that very year (1910) and by Lord Sinha on a later occasion. Still, it must be affirmed that the Act was very drastic and did great mischief during the twelve years it was in operation. It was fatal to the growth of a free and healthy press. It was argued then, as it has been argued since (in 1930, 1932 and 1935) when the Act was revived in the form of Ordinances or Criminal Law Amendment or Special Powers Acts, that no honest journalist had anything to fear and that the free criticism in which the nationalist press indulged was proof conclusive that the press legislation of the Government of India at no time took away the liberty of the press. The apologists are drawn from the class of publicists who find themselves in convenient agreement with the Government on nearly every occasion; on all occasions in fact except when the Government do something agreeable to Indian reformers. They themselves have always been immune from the disagreeable attentions of Government; yes, even when they exceeded all limits of legitimate criticism. One of them once went the length of stigmatizing Lord Morley as "an accomplice in murder", but not a hair of the head of that editor was touched. The point is that there is a vital difference between right and sufferance. Having regard to all the laws on the statute-book, ordinary and special, old and recent, which affect writers and speakers on political subjects I do not hesitate to say that, if we continue to criticize the policies and measures of Government and are yet free, it is by sufferance and not as a matter of legal right. The Government have filled their armoury with weapons with which they can strike us at any time they may choose. We may admire their moderation in not taking them out more frequently than they have done, but the weapons are there and a publicist who forgets their existence does so at his peril.—It should be mentioned here that concurrently with the passing of the Press Act the Bengal public men who had been deported in 1908 were set free after a detention of 14 months without charge, without trial, without reparation.

Annulment of partition

The year 1911 was rendered memorable by the annulment of the partition of Bengal, announced by his Majesty the King-Emperor at the Coronation Durbar in Delhi on December 12 of that year. It was a part of that transaction to remove the capital from Calcutta to Delhi. There were in Bengal those who could not reconcile themselves to the separation of Bihar and Orissa and Chota Nagpur from Bengal or to the removal of the capital. Notwithstanding this, great was the joy of Bengal as a whole that the hated Curzon partition was at last undone. The Congress met that year at Calcutta and the President, Pandit Bishan Narayan Dar, paid a tribute to Bengal on behalf of the whole nation. He said in language of characteristic charm :

> Not only Bengal but the whole of India is most deeply grateful to his Majesty for it; the cause of Bengal is the cause of all India and its triumph marks the triumph of the claims of justice over those of prestige and will go far to strengthen our faith in the efficacy of constitutional agitation carried on in a loyal and law-abiding spirit under British rule. Bengal waged a brave struggle against a great wrong, and it has won a great victory. The victory is due to the justice and righteousness of our rulers, but it is also due to the heroic courage and self-sacrifice of those selfless and patriotic leaders who, through all the storm that raged round them and the clouds of sorrow and suffering that darkened their path,
>
> "Saw the distant gates of Eden gleam,
> And did not dream it was a dream",
>
> who retained their undying faith in their cause and an immovable trust in British justice. They have at last succeeded in the most momentous constitutional struggle of modern India, and have thereby set an inspiring example to the whole nation.

Reference must be made to a tragic incident of December 1912. When Lord Hardinge was making a formal state entry into Delhi, the new capital, a bomb was thrown at him and he received serious injuries. Fortunately they did not prove fatal. It must be said to his credit that this did not embitter him at all. He showed himself to be truly magnanimous and acted with a genuine regard for the interests of India.

The South Africa struggle

During these years, while India was seething with discontent and agitation, the position of our countrymen in South Africa was rapidly deteriorating. There was no thought at all in the minds of either the British or the Boers of rights of citizenship for them. Self-government in South Africa meant and was intended to mean self-government for the minority of white settlers, neither for the Africans nor for the Indian settlers. During the South African war Lord Lansdowne, Secretary of State for War, muttered the accents of righteousness and boldly said that among the many misdeeds of President Kruger's Government none had shocked him more than the ill-treatment of Indians in the Transvaal. This and similar declarations were soon forgotten after the annexation of the two Boer republics. Lord Milner, the High Commissioner in South Africa, was not the man to be humbugged into impartial and sympathetic consideration of the claims of politically powerless Indians. In Lord Courtenay's language he was 'a lost mind'. Step by step the disabilities of the Indians grew more and more intolerable. All the time Mr. Gandhi was fighting a brave fight but with little result. At last he organized on a large scale the passive resistance campaign of 1913. Mr. Gokhale took up the cause in India and with most praiseworthy patriotism the people in India contributed funds generously to enable their brethren in South Africa to carry on the struggle and uphold the honour of the Motherland and the self-respect of her children. Both Mr. Gandhi and Mr. Gokhale showed themselves at their best during that campaign. Still more remarkable, the Viceroy, Lord Hardinge, publicly identified himself with the struggling Indians of South Africa and made a famous declaration that in a situation such as that by which Indians in South Africa were faced passive resistance was both permissible and legitimate as a political method. The struggle ended with a compromise offered by General Smuts, and it was followed by the return of Mr. Gandhi to India. In subsequent years it was alleged that the terms of the compromise had not been honourably kept by the Government of the Union. Certain it is that they continued their anti-Indian policy with unabated rigour. Crisis arose more than once and conferences had to be held to find ways out of them. There has been for some years in South Africa an Agent to the Governor-General of India. The first Agent was the rt. Hon. Srinivasa Sastri. The late Agent, Sir Maharaj Singh, has stated it as his opinion that there was little that the Agent could do and the post might as well be abolished. Successive Agents have done their best in almost forbidding circumstances and all credit should be given to them for their heroic persistence in a forlorn cause. One thing is clear. It has been all the time admitted that for so long as Indians do not enjoy the rights of self-government in their own country it is useless to expect for Indian nationals settled in other parts of the empire or anywhere else in the world the treatment due to them either as British citizens or as civilized men. The history of Indians in South Africa has been repeating itself in East Africa and other parts of the empire. The Government of India have throughout acted almost as a national government in standing up for the Indians settled in other countries and they have achieved a little. But they cannot do much. The Governor-General in Council is subordinate to his Majesty's Government in England and cannot follow any strong policy which may at any time prove embarrassing to his masters in England.

C. F. Andrews

The South African struggle of 1913 first brought into active politics, not on the political issue but on humanitarian grounds, a man whose name cannot be mentioned except with intense admiration, profound respect and deep affection. I allude to my revered friend, Mr. C. F. Andrews. To know Mr. Andrews is to love as well as to respect him. A man with a more complete negation of self or with a larger heart or more free from any sense of race esteem or race prejudice I have not met. The harrowing accounts daily published of the tyrannies inflicted upon the Indians in the 1913 campaign so affected Mr. Andrews' heart—he was at that time a professor in St. Stephen's College, Delhi—that he sought Mr. Gokhale, laid before him a purse of Rs. 1,500 and said, "This is all I have. Please take it and send it to South Africa. I am sorry I have no more." Mr. Gokhale refused to deprive him of what was the whole of his life's savings but requested him to do a greater service still, by proceeding to South Africa and doing there what he could for the struggling Indians. Mr. Andrews, with a companion in the late Mr. W. W. Pearson, forthwith left his position in the college and sailed for South Africa at his own expense. There he came into contact with Mr. Gandhi and since then the Mahatma and Dr. Rabindranath Tagore have been looked up to by Mr. Andrews as his twin *gurus*. There is no part of the world to which he has not gone to help our countrymen. Truly is Mr. Andrews a saint in an age of materialism. It is impossible for Indians to do him too much honour or cherish too much gratitude for him. He is one of those rare persons whose existence saves us from losing faith in humanity.

The War

The great war broke out in the year 1914. The reason authoritatively given for England's participation in it was that she was bound to help Belgium, preserve her neutrality and independence, as she was pledged to do by a treaty of 1839. The Imperial Chancellor of Germany made himself immortal, though not in an honourable sense, by dismissing as a "scrap of paper" that treaty to which Prussia was a party. We in India have occasion to complain that the British Government have in effect treated as scraps of paper many solemn obligations to us. Nonetheless was it to the credit of England that, insufficiently prepared as she was for a great war and though she had no direct or immediate quarrel with Germany or Austria, she resolved to do the right thing in that world crisis. True, British imperial interests were so involved that at some later stage she would have been bound to step on to the arena and she only ante-dated her intervention. Even distant America was forced to come into the war three years later as the result of the unrestricted submarine atrocities to which Germany resorted in sheer desparation. England's participation in the war was a coincidence of duty and interest. Similarly India felt that it was alike her duty and her interest to share with England and other parts of the empire in the gigantic sacrifices which a war of unprecedented magnitude imposed upon the greater part of the world. British statesmen of all parties were profoundly impressed by India's wonderful readiness to make England's cause her own and the most generous expression was given to British sentiments of appreciation and gratitude by responsible statesmen in the two houses of Parliament and outside. They vied with one another in their praise of liberty, equality, justice, international right, self-government, democracy. Mr. Asquith, the Prime Minister, said, "We welcome with appreciation and affection their (Indians') proffered aid and in an empire which knows no distinctions of race or class we all alike are subjects of the King-Emperor and are joint and equal custodians of our common interests and fortunes ....." Viscount Harcourt, Secretary of State for the Colonies, spoke of "the genius of the British race for self-government and good government". Mr. Montagu spoke of the common loyalty of England and India to the ideal of freedom. Other statesmen spoke frequently and emphatically in similar terms. Naturally, expectations were aroused in India that after the conclusion of the war a big step forward would be taken. Mr. Tilak, who was restored to home and liberty soon after the outbreak of the war, appealed to his countrymen to render loyal support to England. Unfortunately the course of progress never does run smooth any more than the course of love, and in the midst of war services and sacrifices and post-war expectations came repression once more. Discontent daily increased as the result of a combination of causes, political and economic, perhaps economic more than political. The Indian Sikhs settled in British Columbia were so badly treated that they came back to this country and swelled the ranks of the discontented. What was called the Komagata Maru incident was a source of great trouble as those who were in active politics at that time will recall. The terrorist movement in Bengal did not abate, rather was gaining strength. The Defence of India Act was passed on the lines of the Defence of the Realm Act in England and the rules under it gave power to Government to intern people without charge or trial. Very free use was made of this power. People began to ask whether this was England's answer to India's loyalty.

Mrs. Besant

In that very year (1914) a new force came into Indian politics. That force was Mrs. Annie Besant. In the activities in which she had taken part in England and in India she had given evidence of her marvellous powers. In her, great intellect and learning were united to an indomitable will, concentrated purposefulness, undaunted courage, indefatigable zeal and a determination never to rest until her work was done. And added to these was her matchless oratory. She did not allow the grass to grow under her feet. She took over a daily newspaper, the old *Madras Standard* named by her *New India*, and day after day she stirred the country by the spoken as well as the written word as scarcely any one else could do. She had the advantage of a ready-made organization in the world-wide Theosophical Society, while the personal devotion to her of thousands of educated men and women was at her disposal to be pressed into service in the new cause which she took up. By temperament she could not be content with the merely ordinary. She soon left many of the old political workers behind in the race and even sneeringly referred to them as " men of yesterday". She started a Home Rule League and under its auspices established organizations throughout the country, distributed vast quantities of propagandist literature and was to be found here, there and everywhere with speeches which always kindled and never restrained. She was interned with Messrs. Arundale and Wadia in the middle of 1917. By this time Mr. Tilak came back to the Congress with his whole following, thanks to amendments in the constitution inserted in 1915 at Bombay. Little was it realized that the presence in the Congress of Mrs. Besant and Mr. Tilak with their large following and strengthened by Lala Lajpat Rai, Mr. C. R. Das and other personalities would result in such a change of policy and method as to make the position of the older leaders and those who followed them impossible in the Congress. This was first realized in that year (1917) and for many of us who could not be persuaded to believe in the efficacy of the tactics of the new gospellors the Congress of 1917 held at Calcutta under the presidency of Mrs. Besant was ominous as showing that it might be our last Congress. And so it turned out to be.

Fresh reforms

In 1916 Lord Chelmsford, the Viceroy, who succeeded Lord Hardinge in the spring of that year, took up the subject of a fresh instalment of constitutional reform. He was in the hands of his advisers, our never-failing friends of the Indian Civil Service, and the consequence was a scheme on every line of which the word " timidity " was written. It was a scheme from which the Indian member of the Executive Council, Sir Sankaran Nair, dissented in a remarkable minute and it was found to be too inadequate even by the

Conservative Secretary of State, Mr. (now Sir Austen) Chamberlain. The result was that the Viceroy invited the Secretary of State to come to India to study the situation on the spot, to confer with him and the Governors and with public men and to evolve a scheme after such consultations. But Mr. Chamberlain suddenly quitted office as the result of the report of the Mesopotamia Commission which severely censured the Government of India for their discreditable ineptitude in the preparation for and the conduct of the military operations in Mesopotamia.

Appointment of Mr. Montagu

Mr. Montagu was then appointed Secretary of State. The appointment was the more significant as, a few weeks earlier in his speech in the Mesopotamia debate in the House of Commons, he uttered an unmeasured denunciation of the Government of India which he described as "wooden and ante-diluvian". Mr. Montagu had been parliamentary under-secretary for India under Lords Morley and Crewe. He was quite unlike other under-secretaries. Although only 31 at the time he first went to the India Office, he showed a keen personal interest in India and quickly mastered her problems. His annual budget speeches in the House of Commons were intellectual treats and embodied lofty sentiments. He came to India in 1912 to acquaint himself personally with the country, her problems and her people. He made many friends and won appreciation by his frank sympathy and progressive outlook. Naturally great hopes were aroused in the Indian mind by the appointment of such a man as his Majesty's Principal Secretary of State for India. At least in this case hope was not belied. The historic Declaration of August 21, 1917, recognizing responsible government as the goal of British policy in India was the first important public act of the new Secretary of State. It was followed the next day by another declaration which removed the bar sinister of race and announced that Indians would thereafter be eligible for the commissioned ranks of the army. His third act was the release of Mrs. Besant and her two associates. He then came to India with a strong delegation, conferred with the Viceroy, the Government of Inida and the governors of provinces, received addresses from deputations of public bodies throughout the country, discussed every important aspect of the constitutional problem with Indians of every variety of opinion and went back to England after six months of hard work and with the Joint Report signed by him and Lord Chelmsford in his pocket. The most important of the deputations and addresses were on behalf of the All India Congress Committee and the Council of the All India Muslim League, which for once had made up their differences and acted jointly. The Joint Report was published in the June following. Unfortunately it was the signal for the further development of the differences between the two sections of Indian Congressmen. They radically differed in their view of the scheme of reforms embodied in the Joint Report. While both recognized defects in it the older party took the view that on the whole it constituted a striking advance over the constitution under which India was then governed, and while pressing for modifications, particularly in the proposals relating to the central government, they held that the best interests of the country required that the scheme should be supported and Mr. Montagu's hands strengthened. The other party took the view that the scheme should be rejected. The most striking expression was given to this opinion by Mrs. Besant in *New India* in the words that it was " unworthy of England to offer and of India to accept". A special session of the Congress was held at Bombay and it passed a resolution condemning the scheme as " inadequate, unsatisfactory and disappointing".

Birth of the Liberal Party

The older party of the Congress were at this stage called upon to decide whether they should or should not join that special session. They conferred among themselves, they gave responsible thought to the question and came to the decision that the country was bigger than the Congress, the Congress was a means to an end whereas the country was the end itself, and at that juncture it was essential that they should not associate themselves with the condemnation of the scheme but should hold a separate conference at which to formulate their own opinions. There were a few who thought that they should not leave the Congress except after actual defeat had made their position untenable. It was not in the mind of even those who took the opposite view permanently to give up the Congress. The course of events, however, perforce converted their temporary abstention into permanent secession. The separate conference of the older party was held at Bombay in the November of that year with Mr. Surendranath Banerjea as President. It was attended by an imposing array of ex-presidents of the Congress and its resolutions embodied detailed and constructive criticism of whatever was unsatisfactory in the Montagu scheme, while at the same time it was frankly recognized that the scheme as a whole must be welcomed.

Government of India Act, 1919

The Government of India Bill based upon the Joint Report was introduced in the House of Commons in the April following. It turned out to be more disappointing than the report. The Liberals, as the ex-Congressmen now described themselves, were not slow to press for a radical amendment of the Bill so as to bring it more into conformity with India's wishes and India's requirements. They went in deputation to England under the leadership of Mr. Surendranath Banerjea and several of them gave evidence before the Joint Select Committee on the Bill. The Congress and the Home Rule League were represented by separate deputations. By this time the latter body under Mrs. Besant's leadership came to take a more favourable view of the Montagu scheme than it had done in the preceding year and in England its delegates, Mrs. Besant and Mr. (now Sir C. P.) Ramaswami Aiyer, and the Liberal delegates acted in close association. The Congress evidence given by Messrs. V. P. Madhava Rao and V. J. Patel alarmed the Joint Committee and was responsible for the latter and unacceptable part of the preamble of the Government of India Act, 1919, which has been reproduced as the preamble of the Act of this year. The Joint Committee included not only Mr. Montagu but Lord Sinha, who had been appointed parliamentary under-secretary for India in the previous December. I can testify from personal observation to the immense labour and the unequalled devotion of both of them and to the enormous pains they took to make the Act acceptable to Indian nationalists to the farthest extent possible in the circumstances. Thanks to Mr. Montagu's combined zeal and ability, the efforts of the Liberal delegation met with a large amount of success. Great is the praise due to Mr. Montagu for all he did.

Mr. Montagu

Mr. Montagu was not an ordinary friend of India. He had a passion for India. I had many opportunities of discussion with him when he was in India and when his scheme was still under preparation. I had accounts from Sir Sankaran Nair, who was then in the Government of India, and from other members of Government, among them Sir George Lowndes and my great friend Sir William Meyer, of the tremendous strength of Mr. Montagu equalled only by his ability and surpassed by his earnestness. In England I had still more opportunities of seeing him at work in the Joint Select Committee and in the India Office. My friend Sir Tej Bahadur Sapru told me of the amount of assistance that he received from Mr. Montagu when he was the Government of India's representative at the Imperial Conference of 1923, where the position of Indians in Kenya and South Africa was considered. As a result of all that I saw and knew and learnt I do not hesitate to give the first place to Mr. Montagu among all the Secretaries of State for India. Greater men had occupied that position, among them Lord Salisbury and Lord Morley. Some earlier and later Secretaries of State—Lord Morley among the former and Mr. Wedgwood Benn among the latter—were undoubted friends of India. But no one before or after Mr. Montagu came anywhere near him in love of India and service of the Indian people. I will repeat that he had nothing less than a passion for India. He died in 1924 a broken-hearted man at the early age of 45 and nothing so pained him as bitter criticism by Indians themselves, the very men in whose service he had spent himself and lost his career. His own countrymen resented what they thought to be his imprudent and unsafe pro-Indianism while the attitude of Indians only served to remind him that there was no gratitude in politics.

Rowlatt Act

I have said that the course of progress never does run smooth. Evidence of this came in abundance in the year 1919. In accordance with the recommendations of what was known as the Rowlatt Committee a bill was introduced in the Legislative Council embodying provisions the most drastic against the liberty of the subject. It aroused the acutest feeling throughout the country and was opposed by every single nonofficial Indian member, elected and nominated included, of the Council but the Government were unrelenting and unbending and employed their official majority to place the Bill on the statute-book. Its operation was limited to three years and the circumstance that even the Government of India had no occasion to put in force a single provision of the Act anywhere in India at any time during those three years, brings into striking relief the wanton unwisdom of the Government's obstinacy in forcing the Bill through in the teeth of a strong, united and determined opposition. What mighty events followed this act of despotism will form the subject of the next section.

Personalities

Bal Gangadhar Tilak

I must now speak of the political personalities of this period. It will be understood that some of those about whom I have already spoken continued their activities during the whole or a part of this period while others of whom I shall now speak were in active public life in the earlier period as well. Among the political leaders who dominated the thoughts and activities of their countrymen during this period the foremost place must be given to Mr. Tilak. He was a born fighter and a typical Mahratta. The passion for freedom was the ruling motive of his life. It was an idea with him that Indians should never express appreciation of anything, however good, done by the Government, for, he said, that would blunt the edge of agitation. For this reason his opinions uttered in public with a political motive, were not always what he held and expressed in private. He was opposed to the Bengal boycott agitation as he thought boycott impossible but was one of its most vehement public advocates. He was satisfied with the Montagu Act but would never say so in public. Gifted with wonderful intelligence, Mr. Tilak brought to bear upon every task that he undertook an iron will and a resolution that nothing could break. There was no means he would not employ to accomplish the task to which he put his hand, to achieve the end upon which he was bent. He was a good master but a bad colleague. The only persons who could get on with him were those who acknowledged his superiority. He found cooperation with equals more difficult than leadership of followers. He had in his Marathi paper, the *Kesari*, a powerful weapon which he never hesitated to wield against anybody who did not adopt his views and follow his ways. There was no man in his day more admired, more loyally followed, or more bitterly hated. The Government looked upon him as the principal enemy of British rule in India. Mr. Montagu told me that he had read the full record of Mr. Tilak's opinions and activities and come to the conclusion that there was only one genuine extremist in India, and that was Mr. Tilak. He suffered for his opinions and activities more than any contemporary politician. But in all circumstances he unflinchingly upheld the banner of freedom for India. He spent himself completely in the furtherance of the cause to which he dedicated his life. No man of his day was more the centre of controversies than Mr. Tilak. But the historian will not fail to recognize that he was one of the men who by indomitable qualities and lifelong service laid the foundation of the future India under Swaraj. Differ as men might, no one, whatever his opinions, could ever think of the national movement in India without thinking of Bal Gangadhar Tilak and giving him a very high place among nation-builders and the makers of New India.

Lajpat Rai

Lala Lajpat Rai dominated the public life of the Punjab. As a member of the Arya Samaj he made great sacrifices for the Dayanand Anglo-Vedic College of Lahore. He was a keen social reformer. He was a journalist. He was an effective orator. As a public speaker I think of Lloyd George and Lajpat Rai together. They had equal capacity for rousing the indignation of the masses. I have heard few speeches which could be placed by the side of Lajpat Rai's speeches in Urdu in the thrilling effect they produced upon the mass mind. Some of his Urdu speeches could only be compared to Mr. Lloyd George's orations at Lime House and Mile End. There was one Congress at which three speeches were made one after another, complementary of one another and each marked by a special quality of its own. It was the Congress held at Patna in 1912. The subject was the position of Indians in South Africa. That year Mr. Gokhale paid a visit to that country to study the question on the spot. He moved a resolution in an English speech of 45 minutes and never had I heard Mr. Gokhale speak with such fluency, such feeling, such animation, such indignation. If almost every one of Mr. Gokhale's speeches was an intellectual treat this particular speech was perhaps more so than almost any other. I never saw Mr. Gokhale so agitated. He was followed by Pandit Madan Mohan Malaviya in a speech in Hindi. He so moved the audience by his most feeling recital of the many tyrannies of which the South African Indians were the victims that nearly everyone who heard him almost shed tears. He made such an appeal to the heart that the heart which was not moved must have been less than human. Pandit Madan Mohan Malaviya was followed by Lala Lajpat Rai in a speech in Urdu and he aroused the passions of the people with such intensity by a speech the most masculine that I thought at the time that if any South African white were anywhere within striking distance his life would not be safe. Lajpat Rai had more than his fair share of hostile Government attentions. He was practically an exile from the country through the whole period of the war and for about a year and a half thereafter. When he was allowed to come back he resumed his normal activities. He wavered from time to time between non-cooperation and parliamentary action. In one respect, however, he completely disagreed with some of his Congress colleagues. He never surrendered Hindu interests. He was as keen upon Hindu-Muslim unity as any one else, but he never believed in the purchase of it by the payment of too heavy a price at the expense of the Hindu community. His death came about in tragic circumstances. He was violently assaulted when participating in the Simon Commission boycott demonstration at Lahore. He did not survive the assault by more than a fortnight. I am among those who believe that his death was hastened thereby. He has left no successor behind in the Punjab and the whole country is the poorer for the loss of such a man.

R. N. Mudholkar

Mr. Mudholkar of Amraoti was another leading public man of those years. He was a convinced moderate. He was a devoted Congressman for 31 years and presided over that session at Patna to which I have referred. I lived with him for more than three years at Amraoti and can say that Mr. Mudholkar was one of the men whose devotion to the interests of the country was genuine and abiding, and he laboured about as hard as any other public man for the amelioration of the condition of his countrymen. He took equally keen interest in politics, education, social reform and industrial development. His own province of Berar never had a more devoted son.

Motilal Ghosh

In Bengal Babus Motilal Ghosh and Aswini Kumar Dutt should be mentioned. The former wielded immense influence through his paper, the *Amrita Bazar Patrika.* He cultivated a style of journalistic criticism which might be said to be unique. No rhetoric, no display of learning, no argument and no language difficult of understanding by the average reader ; but a simple and homely style, only easy words and short sentences : this was Motilal Ghosh's style of writing. What did deadly execution was his stories. He had no equal in the art of holding men up to ridicule by the simple process of telling stories at their expense, and to his stock of stories there was never an end. He was frankly extremist and, seldom as he appeared on the public platform, the influence which he commanded in Bengal was vastly more than that of any other person with the only exceptions of Surendranath Banerjea among men of his day and C. R. Das among those of a younger generation.

Aswini Kumar Dutt

Aswini Kumar Dutt of Barisal, one of the leaders deported in 1908, became a power by the force of character. He had a great belief in education and founded a college in his native town in his father's name. He was profoundly religious and never did anything which was not wholly sincere and honest. In no single public activity did Mr. Aswini Kumar Dutt allow a tinge of selfishness to influence his opinion or action. He had been in the Congress for a score of years before he came into special prominence after the partition of Bengal. Living as he did in East Bengal, which was separated from the main province, he felt the grievance of partition as a personal wrong. He was an eye-witness of the heartless repression that was practised in his province and himself was a victim of official wrath. He was one of the most determined leaders of the anti-partition agitation and in his part of the province his devotion, sacrifice and selflessness made such appeal that his will was the law for the people. Bengal more than any other province depended upon imported foreign salt. In Barisal the boycott was the strongest and shopkeepers would not sell anything foreign including salt. The indigenous commodity could not be had. The collector of the district could not get salt for his table and he had to appeal to Aswini Kumar Dutt to allow a shopkeeper to sell it to him. Aswini Kumar Dutt himself ate his food without salt when he could not get Indian salt. He led a life of dedication and his character and patriotism are written in letters of gold in the annals of Bengal.

Other public men

Sir Rashbehary Ghosh joined the Congress as early as 1886 but did not take an active part in affairs until nearly a score of years later. The most literary of public men, his speeches are delightful reading. Besides, they are marked by ability, judgment and independence. Sir Rashbehary Ghosh and Sir Tarak Nath Palit live in the grateful memory of India by their princely benefactions to Calcutta University.

Lord Sinha was never a great public man, but the story of the period will not be complete without a reference to him. The first man at the bar of the High Court of Calcutta, his power of advocacy was wonderful. I never saw anything to compare with it, except Mr. Gokhale's advocacy of public causes. Lord Sinha made only two appearances on the Congress platform—in 1896 and 1915. He held more eminent official positions than any other Indian, but it is true to say that every one of them came to him unsought while some were forced upon him by friends who would not allow him to decline them. Lord Sinha possessed qualities of intellect and character which rightly won for him both admiration and respect, not less in England than in his own country.

Rao Bahadur G. V. Joshi of Poona was less well known than he deserved. The head master of a Government high school, he yet gave his time to a study of statistics, scientific and detailed, and made himself master of some of the most important of public questions. He used to contribute to the press over the tell-tale initial "J" and not a single letter of his ever escaped attention from any student of public questions. He was of great assistance both to Mr. Ranade and Mr. Gokhale in their work on economics and finance. After retirement he joined Mr. Tilak's party. There is a big volume of his writings and no serious student of Indian affairs can afford to ignore it.

Diwan Bahadur L. A. Govindaraghava Iyar of Madras joined public life in 1901 and early distinguished himself, equally in the Congress and in the Legislative Council. Eloquent as a speaker, sound in judgment, wise in counsel, Mr. Govindaraghava Iyar was deeply religious and excessively charitable—charitable in judgment and charitable with his slender purse. He carried the latter virtue to such excess that the last years of his life were clouded by adversity. I never knew a man more upright, more sincere, more modest. No one could know him without loving and respecting him.

Messrs. Boikunthanath Sen of Berhampore, Ambika Charan Mazumdar of Faridpur and Bhupendranath Basu of Calcutta were three other men who took a leading part in the political activities of the period under review. They had all joined the Congress in its earliest years and gave it their loyal service until the separation came in 1918. Babu Boikunthanath Sen was the chairman of the reception committee of the Congress of 1917 while Babus Ambika Charan Mazumdar and Bhupendranath Basu were its presidents in 1914 at Madras and in 1916 at

Lucknow, respectively. The two latter were vigorous public speakers. Ambika Charan Mazumdar wrote a history of the national movement in his book *Indian National Evolution*. I may be permitted to cite one sentence as a specimen of his oratory. Opposing the Sedition Bill at the Congress held at Amraoti in 1897 Babu Ambika Charan Mazumdar said :

> Gentlemen, for what and for whom should we be seditious ? Is there any shadow of the Moghul still hovering about the country that is beckoning us to raise the Crescent standard on the mouldering walls of Delhi ? Is there a Peshwa in the Deccan who is still harping on the dreams of a Mahratta empire ? Then for whom should we be seditious ?........Gentlemen, born of a people whose ancestors often sacrificed their own children for the supposed welfare of their kings, we disdain to take lessons in loyalty from those whose liberties are bathed and consecrated in royal blood.

Babu Bipin Chandra Pal, also of Bengal, combined in himself the journalist and the orator. He was a great extremist for many years, but in the last half a dozen years of his life parted company with extremism and Congress.—Among other public men of this period were Sir Gangadhar Chitnavis and Sir Bipin Krishna Bose of Nagpur and Sir Narasimha Sarma of this city (Vizagapatam).

The Press

The newspaper press during this period was more handicapped than before by restrictive press legislation. This notwithstanding, the press grew in influence and served the cause of national progress ably and faithfully. The *Hindu* grew from strength to strength in the hands of its new proprietor, Mr. Kasturiranga Iyengar. Diwan Bahadur C. Karunakara Menon edited the *Hindu* for nearly seven years after Mr. Subramania Iyer, under whom he had worked during the previous eight or nine years. He then started a daily paper of his own, the *Indian Patriot*. Unfortunately it did not survive, but during the years of its existence it acquired a high status and was recognized as the most thoughtful paper of its day in the whole country. Mr. Karunakara Menon was one of the men who brought honour to journalism in India. Besides taking over the *Madras Standard,* which she renamed *New India* and conducted as an unflinching daily champion of home-rule, Mrs. Besant founded a splendid weekly paper, the *Commonweal,* which did very good work during the years of its existence. In Bombay Sir Pherozeshah Mehta founded the *Bombay Chronicle* with Mr. B. G. Horniman as its brilliant and resourceful editor, and in the United Provinces Pandit Madan Mohan Malaviya founded the *Leader.* The Punjab and India have been well served throughout the years by the *Tribune* of Lahore. The *Swadesha Mitran* became the popular educator in the Tamil districts, the *Kesari* continued to flourish in the Deccan, and several Bengali newspapers commanded enormous circulations—enormous as circulations go in India. I should not omit to mention the splendid service done to the country through the English columns of the *Gujarati* by Mr. Narayan Vishnu Gokhale, a gentleman every inch of him and a publicist of equal ability and character. He was a staunch Liberal.

CHAPTER IV

(1919-1935)

NON-COOPERATION AND AFTER

Passive resistance

The passing of the Rowlatt Bill brought Mr. Gandhi on the scene. With a faith in passive resistance almost pathetic and incurable, brought over from South Africa, Mr. Gandhi had rehearsed the practice of this art on a smaller scale in connection with local grievances in Bardoli in Gujarat and Champaran in Bihar. The success he achieved there led him to think of the same method on other occasions and on a scale less suited to it. He started the Satyagraha campaign against the Rowlatt Act. He had been warned by some among those whom he consulted that there was such a tremendous amount of anti-British feeling in the country and so little understanding of his own niceties in the practice of Satyagraha, that he would be letting loose forces of disorder which he would be unable to control and in the result the last stage would be worse than the first. He was told by one that in Satyagraha the part of Satya would be only his part, the *agraha* would be practised by others to whom he preached. He brushed aside all objections with a sweep of his hand and embarked upon his campaign. The sequel was far worse than those who had warned him had feared. Riots broke out in Lahore, Amritsar and other places in the Punjab, at Ahmedabad in Gujarat, and elsewhere, in which there was much wanton destruction of life and property and orgies of hooliganism were enacted, which would have been a disgrace to any civilized community. Mr. Gandhi was painfully impressed by what had happened and with a courage all his own he made a public confession that he had made a "Himalayan blunder". Sir Michael O'Dwyer was Lieutenant-Governor of the Punjab. It need not be said that he was not progressive in outlook or excessively sympathetic by nature. First and last he was a vigorous administrator. There was not in his composition a particle of the statesman. He had already exasperated his province by overzeal in the recruitment of men for the war.

If the people committed excesses the Government were not behindhand in doing likewise.

Martial Law

Martial law, which is an euphemism for negation of law, was introduced and it was administered with a harshness and severity which provoked indignation in the whole country. Dyer's exploit at Jallianwala Bagh, Amritsar, was one, if the worst, of a series of acts of brutality. The evidence given before the Hunter Committee of the following year and still more before the Congress Enquiry Committee left no doubt in any one's mind of the lengths to which authority went in hurting and humiliating the people. Sir Sivaswamy Aiyer, who is in the constant habit of weighing his words and of being generous to the opposite side, wrote as follows on the subject* :—

The wholesale slaughter of hundreds of unarmed men at Jallianwala Bagh without giving the crowd an opportunity to disperse, the indifference of General Dyer to the condition of hundreds of people who were wounded in the firing, the firing of machine guns into crowds who had dispersed and taken to their heels, the flogging of men in public, the order compelling thousands of students to walk 16 miles a day for roll-calls, the arrest and detention of 500 students and professors, the compelling of school children of 5 to 7 to attend on parade to salute the flag, the order imposing on owners of property the responsibility for the safety of the martial law posters stuck on their property, the flogging of a marriage party, the censorship of mails, the closure of the Badshahi mosque for six weeks, the arrest and detention of people without

* Introduction to "Martial Law Administration in the Punjab as described by official witnesses". Published by the Madras Liberal League in 1920.

any substantial reason and especially of people who had rendered services to the state in connection with the war fund or otherwise, the flogging of six of the biggest boys in the Islamiah school simply because they happened to be schoolboys and to be big boys, the construction of an open cage for the confinement of arrested persons, the invention of novel punishments like the crawling order, the skipping order and others unknown to any system of law, civil or military, the handcuffing and roping together of persons and keeping them in open trucks for 15 hours, the use of aeroplanes and Lewis guns and the latest paraphernalia of scientific warfare against unarmed citizens, the taking of hostages and the confiscation and destruction of property for the purposes of securing the attendance of absentees, the handcuffing of Hindus and Muhammadans in pairs with the object of demonstrating the consequences of Hindu-Muslim unity, the cutting off of electric and water supplies from Indians' houses, the removal of fans from Indian houses and giving them for use by Europeans, the commandeering of all vehicles owned by Indians and giving them for Europeans for use, the feverish disposal of cases with the object of forestalling the termination of martial law, are some of the many incidents of the administration of martial law, which created a reign of terror in the Punjab and have shocked the public.

Non-cooperation

I referred to the Hunter Committee. It was a committee appointed to enquire into the administration of martial law, with Lord Hunter as chairman. Three Indian members of the committee—Sir Chimanlal Setalvad, Pandit Jagat Narayan and Sir Sultan Ahmad—wrote a minority report. The action taken on the report of the committee was utterly inadequate and failed to give satisfaction. Meanwhile the Treaty of Sevres proposed to dismember Turkey and that kindled the wrath of the Muslims of India. Mr. Gandhi, quick to seize an opportunity, put forward the two, *viz.*, the failure of the Government to do justice to the Punjab and the harsh treatment imposed upon Turkey as reasons for non-cooperation with the Government. At the Congress held at Amritsar in 1919 the question was hotly debated whether Congressmen should cooperate in the working of the new Government of India Act. There both Mr. Gandhi and Mr. Tilak were on the side of cooperation. But Mr. Gandhi later changed his mind. He preached non-cooperation assiduously and in this he found a strong opponent in Mr. Tilak. What course events would have taken inside the Congress and in the country if Mr. Tilak had lived to lead the opposition to Mr. Gandhi can only be a matter of speculation. But the stars favoured Mr. Gandhi. Mr. Tilak died on August 1, 1920, and left no one behind who could be half as formidable an antagonist to the method of non-cooperation. A special session of the Congress was held at Calcutta in September, 1920, under the presidentship of Lala Lajpat Rai to consider the proposal of non-cooperation. Beginning with opposition, Pandit Motilal Nehru became a convert to non-cooperation by the time the Congress took up the resolution. Lala Lajpat Rai was on the whole against non-cooperation in his presidential address, but was less clear in his concluding speech. Pandit Madan Mohan Malaviya and Mr. C. R. Das opposed it right through. They found themselves in a minority and the Congress committed itself to non-cooperation. The result was the abstention of Congressmen from the first elections under the new Act held a couple of months later. Mr. Gandhi's slogan was non-violent non-cooperation. But Congressmen in their zeal interfered in the most objectionable manner—it was not the pure milk of non-violence—in the elections that were held in order to heap trouble and disgrace upon the men who had the temerity to stand as candidates. Their leader was the first man to condemn what he called "slave mentality", but the followers had no use for his nice scruples. Again I speak from personal knowledge when I say that there was no end of non-violent violence or violent non-violence, whichever phrase may be preferred, to embarrass the men who dared to think for themselves and did not possess the "slave mentality" which blindly followed a leader in all his views and ways ; except where their liberty was sought to be restricted by insistence upon righteousness and non-violence. At the

Congress of December, 1920, the resolution of the special session was re-affirmed and non-cooperation became the settled policy of the Congress. At Nagpur Mr. C. R. Das too gave up his dissent and fell into line with the majority.

The Liberals

I said that the older Congressmen's decision to abstain from the special session of the Congress at Bombay in 1918 was not a decision of permanent secession from the Congress but that events forced on them the latter step. The Congress held at Delhi in December, 1918, under the presidentship of Pandit Madan Mohan Malaviya reiterated the resolution of the special session against the Montagu scheme, and in the country there was a raging, tearing campaign against the secessionists which was not calculated to facilitate reunion. The differences of temperament, of outlook, of policy between the two sections emerged into prominence increasingly day by day. Mrs. Besant and Messrs. Govindaraghava Iyar, Srinivasa Sastri and C. P. Ramaswami Aiyer stuck to the Congress for a year more, but their hope that they would be able to ramain there and take back their colleagues proved vain and they too had to leave that organization. Non-cooperation became the official policy of the Congress. The parting of the ways was completed.

The Liberals were attacked then and have been continuously attacked since for what was called an act of desertion. The fact is that to them it was a most painful wrench to separate themselves from the Congress, the national organization of India nursed and reared by the older among them, while the younger ones entered public life as Congressmen and grew up under its auspices. To them patriotism and Congress had been synonymous terms. Is it in human nature that they would have taken a step so painful to them except under a sense of compelling public necessity ? To say the contrary is to deny the attributes of human nature. They knew what they were letting themselves in for and, with a full consciousness of the unpopularity which would be their portion, they yet acted as their judgment and their conscience bade them do in the interests of the country as they understood them and in the service of the cause to which they had given the best in them. I say every word of this with complete personal knowledge as one of the men who had to take the unpleasant decision. All sorts of disreputable motives have been attributed to the Liberals for their separation from the Congress. But this is part of the business of the day for public men and harsh words break no bones. What is of importance is that a public man should have character. This quality was once defined as "completely fashioned will". I conceive that for a man or a body of men to seem to be what they are not, to affect opinions which they do not hold, to subscribe to policies in which they disbelieve is far more demoralizing to the individual, far more detrimental to the growth of honest and wholesome public opinion and far more injurious to the country than for men honestly to act in accordance with their convictions. No thoughtful man can commend the hypocrisy that is involved in outward conformity with inward dissent. I was a Congressman for twenty years and have been a Liberal for seventeen. In the latter period I have not once been conscious of uttering an opinion or doing an act which I had not or would not have uttered or done in my Congress days. And what I say of myself my fellow-Liberals can say of themselves. If Liberals today are not members of the Congress they are still Congressmen in the sense in which they were, and that is enough for them. Herbert Spencer put the case very well for the guidance of public men when he said that men should do what they deemed to be right : "If public approbation comes well and good; if it does not come, also well and good, though not nearly so well and good." Liberals are human and value the good will of their countrymen. But conscience and judgment come above public approbation. Merely to seek popularity has been recognized by competent judges as about the worst fault of which a public man can be guilty. In the light of all that has happened in the Congress and in the country during the last sixteen years no Liberal to-day need apologize or doubt or hesitate. If there was a doubt at the beginning whether Liberals acted rightly the events that have followed one another in quick succession constitute, they are convinced, their complete vindication.

Non-cooperation and repression

Mr. Winston Churchill wrote with reference to Ireland that reforms planted under the shadow of coercion could have but a sickly growth. It has been the irony of fate that in India reform and repression seem to have contracted an unholy alliance. Agitation and repression were in full swing when the first councils were established under the Act of 1909, and it has been seen that the Press Act was the first product of the new Indian Legislative Council's activity. The Montagu Act of 1919 was preceded by the Rowlatt Act, the Satyagraha campaign and the martial law administration, and it was followed by the non-cooperation movement. When the first Councils under the Montagu Act met at the beginning of 1921 the country was full of unrest and feelings ran so high that every person who was an elected member of any legislative council was disliked and distrusted, while the few who accepted office as ministers or members of executive councils came in for special opprobrium. The introduction of the new constitution was preceded by a gracious Royal Proclamation and an amnesty to political prisoners. These, however, had no healing effect as the memory of the martial law atrocities was fresh in the public mind. Inaugurating the Chamber of Princes and the new central legislature, his Royal Highness the Duke of Connaught publicly expressed regret for the Punjab excesses and he read a message from the King-Emperor definitely recognizing Swaraj in the sense of Dominion Status as the goal of British policy. But no impression was made on the Congress and the pro-Congress mind. The non-cooperation agitation was carried on intensively throughout the country. Boycott of councils, courts of law and schools and colleges—what was called the triple boycott—, the picketing of liquor shops, the establishment of Panchayats and of national schools were the main planks of the Congress platform. Less important items such as the relinquishment of honorary offices and of titles and the boycott of all official functions need only be mentioned. The temper of the people was roused. Open contempt was preached for law, authority was undermined. There were sporadic disturbances in different parts of the country. While Hindu-Muslim unity was on the lips of every Congressman and while Mahatma Gandhi and the brothers Shaukat Ali and Mohammad Ali were fraternizing with each other came the most rude shock of the Moplah disturbance in Malabar in which the Hindus fared the worst. His Royal Highness the Prince of Wales visited India in the cold weather of 1921-22. Congress preached a boycott of that visit and the preaching was enforced by practical action. The day on which his Royal Highness landed at Bombay was disgraced by a bloody riot of which Mr. Gandhi himself said that what he had seen stank in his nostrils. This riot was followed by instructions by the Government of India to all local Governments to repress without hesitation. All the powers which the law conferred were to be unhesitatingly used and if they were found to be inadequate, whatever more powers were needed by the executive government would be given them. Congress volunteers were declared to be an unlawful body. The people's answer to this was to enlist themselves as volunteers in larger numbers. They were sent to jail by the thousand, among them being such leaders as Mr. C. R. Das and Pandit Motilal Nehru. The authorities were hard put to it to prevent the outbreak of riots at places which the Prince of Wales was to visit. When thousands of educated men were being imprisoned, it was in the nature of things impossible for the royal visit to evoke popular enthusiasm. Cause and effect were inextricably mixed up. A way out of the impasse was sought when Lord Reading, the Viceroy, was persuaded—principally by his then Law Member, Sir Tej Bahadur Sapru—to agree to a round table conference at which spokesmen of the Government and the people might talk matters over. Not only Sir Tej Bahadur Sapru, but Pandit Madan Mohan Malaviya on the side of the Congress actively exerted himself to see the suggested conference materialize. Mr. C. R. Das was eager to seize the opportunity and that year's President of the Congress, Mr. C. Vijiaraghavachariar, was of the same opinion. So were several other Congress leaders. But Mr. Gandhi put his veto. The situation grew from bad to worse. Mr. Das was the President-elect of the Congress which met at Ahmedabad, but he was in jail and Hakim Ajmal Khan, a patriot equally respected by Hindus and Muslims, by Liberals and Congressmen, was improvised as acting President. The answer of the Congress to Government's repression was to go farther in the direction of extremism. The creed of the Congress was altered, for the worse as non-Congressmen thought. Among those who unexpectedly signed the new creed was Pandit Madan Mohan Malaviya. That Congress declared for civil disobedience and appointed Mr. Gandhi as dictator. Things grew from bad to worse after the session of the

Congress. Violence was becoming increasingly frequent. Its culmination was the savage riot at Chaurichaura in the Gorakhpur district of the United Provinces. In the Gorakhpur division no action had been taken under the Criminal Law Amendment Act and the commissioner took pride in the fact that he had been able to keep the peace in all his three districts without recourse to any special law, and he advised the Government to withdraw the notification under the Criminal Law Amendment Act from the whole of his division. What must have been his mortification to find but six or seven days later Chaurichaura confound him with a vengeance! The brutality of this riot so went home to Mr. Gandhi's heart that he declared for the abandonment or suspension of the non-cooperation movement and the substitution in its place of what was called the constructive programme. After Chaurichaura non-cooperation ebbed and with its suspension there grew up inside the Congress, men who wanted that Congressmen should enter the legislatures and "non-cooperate from within" by "consistent, continuous and persistent obstruction". It must be mentioned here that by this time Mr. Gandhi had been sent to jail and so were the brothers Mohammad Ali and Shaukat Ali. Messrs. C. R. Das and Motilal Nehru came out of jail. They apparently felt that they had made a sacrifice for nothing and that some other means must be found to make their position felt by the Government. It was clear by then that intensive repression had done its work only too well. Before, however, a change of programme was finally decided upon the All India Congress Committee constituted a committee for "the further consideration of the question whether civil disobedience in some form or some other measure of a similar character should be adopted". Hakim Ajmal Khan was the president of the committee and its members were Mr. Motilal Nehru, Dr. Ansari, Mr. C.

Rajagopalachariar, Mr. V. J. Patel and Mr. S. Kasturiranga Iyengar. (The report was drawn by Mr. Nehru.)

Civil Disobedience Enquiry Committee

The report of the Civil Disobedience Enquiry Committee was quite instructive. It was certainly a one-sided document as it was bound to be in the nature of things. But there was in it enough to enable uncommitted men to draw non-partizan conclusions. It was "admitted that so far as effort was directed to the weaning of students from Government schools and colleges, it has met with poor success" and that the majority of the students who had come out of Government schools were "obliged to return gradually to their old schools": which does not appear exactly to support the claim later made in the report that the non-cooperation movement "has destroyed the prestige of Government institutions".

Admission of failure

While "the unfortunate paucity of national institutions" was deplored it was admitted that the condition of such institutions as existed "is far from satisfactory", "in most cases the syllabus of studies is identical with that of the Government institutions (this will be marked) with the exception of the *charkha*, handloom and compulsory learning of Hindi". "Almost every institution visited by us was in financial distress". The committee recommended a suspension of "all active propaganda calling upon boys to come out of schools and colleges". But propaganda was again carried on in this behalf during the civil disobedience campaign of 1930, propaganda accompanied by picketing, which in some cases was intensive as well as offensive. But very little success attended this renewed effort to seduce from their allegiance to schools and colleges young men in their teens who had still to cut their wisdom teeth. And one is constrained to smile at the note of triumph struck by the experienced authors of the report at the enthusiasm of such young men for their movement. The attempt was not repeated in the second civil disobedience campaign of 1932. As regards the boycott of courts the report says that " it must, as in the case of students, be admitted that this item of the programme has failed " and that while the number of lawyers who suspended practice in courts " is insignificant compared to their full strength " " it has now been further reduced by some of them having gone back to practice for private and other reasons". The special pleading of the committee in favour of lawyers does not affect the fact which they admitted. Panchayats were to be substituted for courts of law, as national schools were to be for government institutions. The admission of the failure of the latter attempt was followed in the report by the confession that " on the whole the attempt to have any proper substitute for the existing courts has undoubtedly failed". What oppression was practised by some of these Panchayats was a matter of public knowledge at that time and may still be recalled by those whose memories are not too short. Another admission related to *khaddar*. " Indeed " the committee said, " it has now become impossible to say with certainty of any particular piece that it is *shudh khaddar* " and that " not many of the numerous *khaddar bhandars* dotting the whole country deal exclusively in the genuine stuff". " It cannot be said of any district or tahsil that 'therein a vast majority of the population have adopted full Swadeshi or are clothed out of cloth handspun and handwoven and believe in and practise all the other items of non-cooperation'." The picketing of liquor shops was an item in the non-cooperation programme which was attended with much unpleasantness and at least some sporadic disturbances. Was it a success from the point of view of the Congress ? Here is the answer given by the committee : "The immediate effect was a marked decline in the consumption of liquor, but after the removal of the pickets the pendulum swung back and the evil asserted itself again in full force." It is notorious that the Government made a far too free use of sec. 144 of the Criminal Procedure Code; that it was employed for purposes for which it had not been intended. But by the side of this must be placed a significant observation of the committee. They said: "It is not the case that all orders under sec. 144 are invalid; if that were so, sec. 144 would be superfluous which it certainly is not."

Boycott of councils

It will be recalled that the boycott of councils played a very large part—I might say the dominant part—in the Congress activities of the autumn of 1920. Councils like courts of law were things "impure", "unclean," "unholy," the very touch of which was "pollution". This item of the programme formed the subject of most careful consideration by the committee. The result was an equal division of opinion among the members. While Dr. Ansari (who has changed his opinion since last year) [1] and Messrs. Kasturiranga Iyengar and Rajagopalachariar were for maintaining the boycott, Hakim Ajmal Khan, Pandit Motilal Nehru and Mr. V. J. Patel took the contrary view. The latter said that the boycott contemplated by Mr. Gandhi was "the wholesale abstention of voters from voting; he had hoped to keep councils empty". It would appear that the boycott of councils had been agreed to in the first instance under the influence of Mr. Gandhi's promise of "Swaraj within twelve months". But the three members who were for re-entry into councils wrote: "Times have now changed. Circumstances have altered. The period of the struggle is indefinitely prolonged." They further wrote:

Measures affecting the daily life of the people are being enacted year

1 Dr. Ansari has since passed away.

after year. Fresh taxation and huge liabilities are being imposed and will continue to be imposed with the help and in the name of the so-called representatives of the people and, *nolens volens*, the people will have to submit to them. Under these circumstances it is a question for consideration how far the hold of the Congress over the masses can remain unaffected.

Suppose the Congress persists in the boycott of the councils in its present form and it is found that a greater percentage of voters record their votes on this occasion, our claim would be discredited. We are inclined to believe that this policy of abstention has lost its charm and it is not at all unlikely that a greater percentage of voters will poll at the ensuing elections. In that event the success gained at the last elections will be a thing of the past and the whole movement might be adversely affected.

Their conclusion was stated in the following eloquent passage :—

Before you are able to clothe a millionth part of the vast population in India in hand-spun and hand-woven *khaddar,* before you can supply an infinitesimal fraction of the demand for national educational institutions, before any appreciable progress can be made in the removal of untouchability, before you can extricate yourself from the vicious circle which has effectively frustrated your efforts to restore inter-communal unity, we warn you that you will have completely gone under, unless you open your eyes to the present need of the hour. Theories and dogmas are all very well in their own way, but they will not carry you far if you ride them to death. Knock these councils on the head and you will accomplish what millions spent in foreign propaganda cannot achieve. Wreck the reforms and you will smash at one blow the huge superstructure of world-wide deception which has cost millions to build up.

Lastly, the advocates of council entry urged it on the ground that it was "a practical and desirable measure of a character similar to civil disobedience". "Of a character similar to civil disobedience"! Self-deception, thy name is—

These three gentlemen innocently believed that if only they went in they were certain "to smash the councils" and "wreck the reforms". "We shall enter the councils to end them, as they cannot be mended as we wish them to be." As if ending them were child's play ! A most instructive paragraph of the report is paragraph 109 on "sweeping changes effected". In that paragraph a chronological account was given of the numerous changes in the Congress programme made between 1919 and 1922.

The other three members contended that "the constitution of seats in the legislative council with its class, communal and special interests renders it absolutely impossible to secure a majority sufficient to create deadlocks in the manner contemplated". They further wrote :

> When the proposal was discussed in 1920 Mahatma Gandhi deprecated it on the ground that it was not a good and honest policy to get entrance into an institution in order to wreck it. Further, every member is required to take the oath of allegiance which includes a solemn promise 'faithfully to discharge the duty upon which he is about to enter'. No conscientious person can stand for election with the avowed object of wrecking the institution and take such an oath, and except by causistry or mental reservation can feel justified in adopting such a course. Indiscriminate obstruction must be a manifest violation of the oath and it should be repellant to every sincere believer in the basic principles of the non-cooperation movement.

To one whose considered opinion was opposed to the whole of this new programme as being wholly misconceived this record of changes is pathetic. The "triple boycott" having been finished, an internecine struggle ensued between Swarajists as the council entry section styled themselves, and the no-changers as the others were called. In the struggle the two principal lieutenants of Mr. Gandhi, Messrs. C. R. Das and Motilal Nehru, led the council entry section. Those opposed to them had no comparable leader, the Mahatma being still in jail. A special session of the Congress was held at Delhi in the autumn of 1923 to get sanction for Congressmen to seek election. It was obtained and in the elections that followed Congress candidates achieved great success in a majority of provinces. There was a trial of strength between the no-changers and the Swarajists after Mahatma Gandhi's return from jail. The latter triumphed, and Mahatma Gandhi helped them thereafter.

Swarajists in the legislature

Notwithstanding their great electoral successes the Swarajists were not in a majority in almost any council. But by a judicious combination with members of other parties they succeeded in putting an end to ministries in Bengal and the Central Provinces. In other legislative bodies there was on a majority of occasions agreement between and joint action by Congress and other nationalist members. The work of the legislatures afforded convincing proof that the points of agreement among Indian nationalists of one party and another are far more than any differences. This was anticipated by the Civil Disobedience Committee. It was said in the committee's report:

> A good deal has been said about fundamental differences of principles (among the various schools of thought in India), but those principles themselves relate only to methods and do not affect the essentials....Making every allowance for such differences....we think there will be left a substantial residuum of good and solid work in which all parties can join without any sacrifice of principle. We are conscious that the irresistible logic of facts has compelled us to say some hard things about the general attitude of councillors and cooperators throughout the country, but we must not be understood to mean that all councillors and cooperators are alike. Many of them have undoubtedly tried their best to work, if on lines of cooperation, in the right spirit.....We venture to think that while agreeing to differ where difference is unavoidable it is possible to discover a common basis for joint action if both parties meet in the right spirit. A beginning, however small, once made, is bound to lead to very desirable results..... As it is the highest duty of a non-cooperator to cooperate with his own countrymen where possible, we trust that those indications will develop into definite proposals at no distant date.

Congress attitude towards non-Congress nationalists

It is to be regretted that this wise conception of public duty was completely forgotten by Congressmen in every election in which they took part. Even after actual experience of council work had demonstrated to the satisfaction of Congress M. L. A.'s and M. L. C.'s that they had derived strength from the cooperation of other nationalist members, that in fact they would have achieved little success in the absence of such cooperation, every time they declared war upon non-Congressmen without reference to their character or antecedents. This point need not be elaborated as our latest experience is as recent as last year. The experiment was once tried in the British House of Commons of a combination of cooperation inside Parliament concurrently with war in the constituencies [1]. The experiment failed disastrously. I cannot help thinking that Congressmen, individuals excepted, have come to regard themselves as supermen and developed a degree of contemptuous intolerance for those who do not swear by their very frequently changing dogmas and " doxies " and that they have not always been able to resist the temptation of placing party above country.

Violation of parliamentary principle

Congress candidates for the legislature were required to pledge themselves to act always in obedience to mandates that they might receive from the authorities of the Congress. The basic principle of parliamentary government is that elected members are responsible to their constituencies and not to an authority outside the legislature and unrelated to constituencies. Mr. J. A. Spender characterized this as a " subversive and anti-parliamentary doctrine". The Labour party in England tried the same method in 1924 when the first Labour Government was in office. They partially succeeded in forcing it upon the Government. The result was the defeat of the Government within ten months of taking office.

'Patriotism in locomotion'

Having failed, as they were bound to do, in their ambition to " smash " or " end " the councils and " wreck the reforms ", Congress legislators made a brave show of a staged walk-out from all legislative bodies in March, 1926. But from council after council were received appeals from Congress members for permission to walk in again on the ground of the special importance of certain subjects.

1. The reference is to the relations between the Labour and Liberal parties in 1924.

In order not to lose their hold over their members the central Congress executive went on giving such permission wherever it was applied for. Between March, 1926, and the dissolution of the then Assembly and councils it was a regular scene, Congressmen walking in and walking out for reasons best known to themselves. They were characterized by one Finance Member in the United Provinces as "peripatetic patriots" while Sir Tej Bahadur Sapru described their theatricalities as "patriotism in locomotion".

They all stood for election again in 1926, but this time, at least some of them found that the gilt was off the ginger bread. Electors were confused by the walk-in—walk-out policy. They could not be sure whether Congress members would stick to their seats and do their duty, and they saw that the councils, far from being smashed or ended were flourishing ; Congressmen themselves vying with one another to re-enter them. There was another obstacle to a repetition of the dramatic success of 1923. During those three years Congressmen succeeded in producing on the Hindu mind the impression that Hindu interests, wherever they clashed with Muslim, were not safe in Congress hands. The length to which some Congress leaders were prepared to go to propitiate Muslims was shown by the "pact" concluded in December, 1923, by Mr. C. R. Das with the Muslims of Bengal. It was furiously denounced by Bengal Hindus and condemned by Hindu public opinion generally in the whole country, Congress Hindus included. Therefore the Hindu Mahasabha entered the lists and under the leadership of Pandit Madan Mohan Malaviya and Lala Lajpat Rai, achieved striking successes. In the councils elected that year the Congress element was distinctly weaker than in the preceding councils. Again there was almost complete cooperation, as I can say from direct knowledge, among them,

Liberals and other nationalists. Always, however, cooperation ended when an election was on. The Congress members were again called out during the lifetime of those councils and subsequently they were asked to resign. They went back last year to the Assembly and will return to the provincial legislatures at the next election. It is a curious commentary upon the soundness of the initial policy of boycott of councils that no less a man than Mahatma Gandhi himself should have declared, as he did a few months ago, that the parliamentary mentality had come to stay in the Congress, and that he himself should have actively supported re-entry into councils although some of his more devoted followers could not be persuaded to this way of thinking.

The Akali movement

In those years (1921-24) great stir was made in the Punjab by the Sikh movement, the Akali, against another section of Sikhs, the Udasi. The agitation was modelled on the Congress Satyagraha, and the Government of the Punjab dealt with it by the familiar method of repression. The law was certainly broken by the Akalis but it is equally undoubted that the Government method of handling them was marked by excess of harshness and altogether left much to be desired. The trouble went on during the flabby regime of Sir Edward Maclagan in the Punjab. But a master-mind [1] took his place in 1924 and was quickly able to find a solution, not by coercion but by consent. The Congress, or Congressmen, took the side of the Akalis, it may be assumed less because of appreciation of the merits of the dispute between them and the Udasis than because the former came into conflict with the Government. It is noteworthy and significant that wherever there has been trouble in the land, on any matter and for whatever

1. Sir Malcolm (now Lord) Hailey.

reason, Congressmen have nearly always been soon on the spot on the side of the party that caused the trouble, provided it was against the Government or capitalists or landlords. Well might they say, "I bring not peace but the sword"[1].

Civil disobedience

Organized mass civil disobedience was embarked upon in 1930 and again in 1932. What the result has been need not be stated. The patron-saint of this political method publicly declared last year that he was convinced that he alone in the whole country was qualified and competent to practise civil disobedience. How one could wish that this discovery had been made by him before and not after he had led tens of thousands of people to jail and disturbed the whole political situation. So the end of it all—passive resistance, Satyagraha, non-cooperation, triple boycott, mass civil disobedience—is that the principal concern of Congressmen today, after and as the result of their various experiences, is to find the largest possible number of places for themselves in legislative councils. The only difference between them and the much abused Liberals is that the latter were able to anticipate what Congressmen could only learn by repeated and bitter experience. Lord Rosebery defined statesmanship as the foresight of commonsense. I will not emphasize the application of this definition to Indian political parties.

Congressmen and office

At the present moment Congressmen are finding it the most difficult question to decide whether they should or should not accept office in provinces where the elections may place them in a position to form governments. I earnestly hope that the decision of the Congress will be in the

1. This paragraph was not in the lecture as delivered.

affirmative.[1] It is quite certain that all hope of wrecking the councils is futile. The councils will be so constituted as to make this impossible. The utmost that can be attempted by any individual or party is to do such work in office or in opposition as will produce the maximum result, firstly to promote the well-being of the people and secondly—this is not less important than the first—to facilitate substantial amendments of the unacceptable constitution that has been imposed upon us, so that the advent of Swaraj may be accelerated.

The Government of India and the Legislative Assembly did good work in 1922 in repealing the Press Act of 1910 and some other repressive laws. The credit for this must be given chiefly to the then Law Member, Sir Tej Bahadur Sapru, who presided over the committee which enquired into the subject.

Princes' Protection Acts

Unfortunately the repeal of the Press Act was soon followed by the Princes' Protection Act, and one more Act has since been passed for their "protection". "Protection" from whom and from what? In the vast majority of states even elementary political rights are denied to the people. They have no right of public meeting, no free press, no representative institutions, no independent judiciary. The Indian States People's Conference has to assemble in British India. For the ventilation of grievances the people of the states have to depend in the main upon the press of British India. The princes as a whole have given no evidence of a change of political mentality. Every time they insist upon the retention of absolute power in their hands. Yet, far from persuading them to redress the grievances of their subjects and to grant to them a modicum of political

1. And so has it been.

rights, the Government of India have twice come to their rescue by means of legislative measures to "protect" them from criticism in the press of British India.

Kenya

In the year 1923 India was agitated by a new policy in Kenya directed against the Indian settlers there. It was a policy so anti-Indian that the rt. hon. V. S. Srinivasa Sastri of all the people in the world was compelled to think aloud of the necessity of India seeking a destiny outside the empire and he advocated the boycott of the British Empire Exhibition of that and the following year. The good work done by Sir Tej Bahadur Sapru on this and the twin subject of the position of Indians in South Africa at the Imperial Conference held in London during that autumn must be mentioned.

Communal relations

The year 1924 saw bloody communal riots in several parts of the country, in particular in Delhi and the United Provinces. Mahatma Gandhi was so oppressed by these outbreaks, after all that had been said on Hindu-Muslim unity in connection with the non-cooperation movement, that he resolved to fast for a number of days. This led to the convening by Mr. Mohammad Ali as the Congress President of that year, in cooperation with Swami Shraddhanand, of a unity conference in Delhi. It was largely attended. Earnest discussions took place. The most excellent spirit prevailed on both sides. The Metropolitan himself attended and blessed the conference. Yet there was no result. It was a conference in which both Congressmen and Liberals, the Muslim League as well as the Hindu Mahasabha, took part. Shortly after, a drastic ordinance was promulgated in Bengal for dealing with the terrorist movement and many persons including Mr. Subhas Chandra Bose were interned. This was the occasion for another conference of all the parties in Bombay. A committee was appointed there, with Mahatma Gandhi as chairman and Mr. Motilal Nehru as secretary, to consider in detail how inter-communal harmony could be promoted and unity between political parties brought about. The committee met in Delhi in January, 1925, under the chairmanship of Mahatma Gandhi. Having started with the Hindu-Muslim question it ended with it. Protracted deliberations followed for a whole week. Again the deliberations proved infructuous. In that committee I was able personally to witness for the first time a suppressed revolt among prominent Congressmen against the ideas of Mahatma Gandhi and Messrs. C. R. Das and Motilal Nehru. The communal tension was not eased. The Calcutta riots of 1926, the riots at Dacca, the riots in Bombay, repeated riots in the United Provinces, of which the culmination was the disastrous Cawnpore riot of 1931—all proclaimed trumpet-tongued that there was no Hindu-Muslim unity. In the United Provinces one Governor almost boasted in his farewell speech that he had had to deal with no fewer than 83 communal riots during his five years !

Hindu Mahasabha

This communal tension increased the activities of the Hindu Mahasabha, which had existed for years before, without however becoming conspicuous as a public body that had to be reckoned with. More Hindu leaders joined its ranks. But it derived its strength principally from the feeling among the Hindus that they were not getting a square deal. Rightly or wrongly, they think and feel that there is in the policy and measures of Government and in the attitude of their officers something which is not conducive to the advancement of the Hindu community. They are blamed for being communalists and there are many critics—and not only among non-Hindus—to whom the very existence of the Mahasabha appears to be an offence. Curiously enough, the identical view is not taken of the Muslim League and other Muslim organizations. The Congress itself in 1916 treated the Mahasabha with scant courtesy by refusing to give its representatives a hearing when discussions were in progress between the Congress Committee and the Council of the Muslim League which resulted in the so-called Lucknow Pact. Among Hindu political leaders, all of them nationalists, there were several in earlier years who favoured the establishment of Hindu Sabhas and joined them where they were started. Among them were Pandit Bishan Narayan Dar, Babu Ganga Prasad Varma and Sir Tej Bahadur Sapru. Some of them are no more, a few have changed their opinions. Similarly, some who had not been convinced of the expediency of a Hindu communal organization were in later years converted to the opposite view and have since joined the Mahasabha. In the Punjab, however, where the communal issue has ever been to the fore, Hindu leaders without exception were members of the Hindu Sabha, including such men as Swami Shraddhanand, Sir Pratul Chatterji, Rai Bahadur Kali Prasanna Roy, Rai Bahadur Lal Chand, Lala Lajpat Rai and Sir Shadi Lal. After the Punjab comes Bengal in this line of thought and activity. One Punjabi leader[1] went so far as to speak of the (Hindus') "weakening desire for unity" (with Muslims), while Swami Shraddhanand's opinion was, "Hindu-Muslim unity may be the result but will not be the cause of Swaraj". But outside the Punjab it was thought at one time, and for long, that the Congress was there and there should be no Hindu organization. What view the present-day Congress takes of Hindu-Muslim questions not excepting even the communal "award" is a fact too recent to need special

1. The late Rai Bahadur Lal Chand in 1908.

15

mention. The question is whether, consistently with our larger national allegiance and our efforts to attain Swaraj, it is or is not the duty of the Hindus, in the situation as it has developed in recent years and is today and threatens to be at least for some time yet, to bestow a thought on the requirements of their community. Let it be remembered that Muslim communal organizations are in full vigour and strength. The continued existence of separate communal electorates is a far more important fact. The tone and direction given to activities inside legislative councils on communal issues by the presence in them of members owning separate allegiance to their different communities, he who runs may read. The nature of the coming constitution may justly lead people to apprehend that in the near future communal unity is not likely to reign supreme in the country. I consider myself to be about as good a nationalist as any in the country. But I cannot forget and do not want to forget that I am a Hindu and that it is my duty as a public man to exert myself in defence of the interests of Hindus as an integral part of the Indian nation. I am quite sure my co-religionists in general feel as I do. Mr. Birrell's observation is apposite, *viz.*, that while it is bad to be oppressed by a majority it is worse to be oppressed by a minority. In all the circumstances, I do feel convinced of the necessity of a strong and representative organization of the Hindu community, not with offensive intent or in a spirit of communal bigotry, but wholly for defensive purposes and with complete fidelity to the national ideal. The danger should be guarded against of its getting into the hands of what for want of a better word may be called fanatics. Their over-zeal is not a service to the community. And it deters moderate men who can be useful, from identifying themselves with that body.

Hindu disunity

It is unfortunate that the age-old weakness of the Hindu community to be a house divided against itself has not disappeared under the stress of modern necessities. While Musalmans almost to a man act as a unit whenever they feel rightly or wrongly that their communal interests are in jeopardy, Hindus have never done so. The greatest of Muslim landed magnates make common cause with the humblest of their co-religionists and join in representations to Government in their behalf, but a large number of Hindu zamindars would not publicly associate themselves with their aggrieved co-religionists lest thereby they offend the Government. Among Hindus of the middle class the sentiment of nationalism deters not a few from coming forward as spokesmen of their community. I have reason to think that the majority of Hindu officials have an idea that, if they even do bare justice to their co-religionists, they are likely to be stigmatized as being anti-Muslim as well as to displease their official superiors and therefore, they are prone to go out of their way to stretch a point or two in favour of the other community. The differences between the advocates and the opponents of social reform also militate against united action. Dissatisfied with the progressive attitude of the Hindu Mahasabha on questions of social reform, the more orthodox have started a separate organization of their own. For a wonder, they appropriate to themselves the designation of Sanatanists, as if there were in the customs and institutions to which they tenaciously cling anything *sanatan* ! A consideration of the *rationale* of the caste system would not be relevant to the subject of these lectures. But this may be said. The *caste spirit* carried into secular public affairs has not only nothing to justify or even excuse it but is daily proving most harmful to the community as a whole.

It is an ironic tragedy that this objectionable spirit is betrayed even by persons who in their daily lives have openly discarded every restraint imposed by the rules of caste.

The Non-Brahman movement

The non-Brahmans of Madras, followed by those of Bombay and the Central Provinces, have in recent years organized themselves on the basis of non-Brahmanism which has often degenerated into anti-Brahmanism. Their organization in Madras is called the Justice party. With the ostensible object of obtaining justice for themselves the non-Brahmans of the Justice party have not hesitated to advocate as well as do gross injustice to Brahmans. This division of the Hindu community into Brahmans and non-Brahmans carried into the political sphere is another and a patent source of weakness to the community as a whole. Curiously enough, non-Brahmans, including those who belong to the so-called Justice party, are not more just or liberal to the depressed classes than the Brahmans who are their pet aversion. The non-Brahman movement is limited to non-Brahman caste Hindus. This was stated in evidence before the Joint Select Committee of 1919 on behalf of the Justice party.

Can the Government of Madras be wholly acquitted of partiality for the non-Brahman movement which has found concrete expression in the Justice party ? I fear not. An illuminating piece of evidence was furnished during the examination by Lord Sinha of Sir Alexander Cardew, who was so prominent in the Government of Madras in those years, before the Joint Select Committee on the Government of India Bill of 1919. Sir Alexander having emphatically denied that the Government of Madras had at any time done anything to stimulate the growth of the Justice party, Lord Sinha confronted him with a passage in an official resolution which bore the signature " A. G. Cardew " with the result that the witness had to look small and give up his assertiveness. The examination of Sir K. V. Reddy by Mr. Montagu before the same Committee was equally interesting and suggestive in this connection.

Untouchability

To treat any human beings as untouchables is a grotesque travesty of religion, yet millions of them have been so treated for centuries. Those neglected people are now having their revenge on the community which has ill-treated them. The removal of untouchability and the elevation of the depressed classes by means of education and economic development has always been a main plank in the platform of the social reformer. But it is true to say that vitality has been imparted to the movement by the supreme effort of Mahatma Gandhi. The fullest political advantage has been taken of the existence of the depressed classes by those well-wishers of India who are eager to postpone, till Doomsday in the afternoon if they could, self-government for India. There are depressed classes among Mahomedans and Christians too—the former was admitted in the Legislative Council by the Muslim Minister in the United Provinces [1]—but their existence is ignored in political discussions. It cannot be without meaning that in census after census the numbers of the classes called depressed show a marvellous increase. And let it be remembered that it was a British official who was census commissioner, Mr. (afterwards Sir Edward) Gait, who for the first time gave instructions that in the census returns the depressed classes should be shown as being separate from other Hindus. I am not concerned here and now with the theatrical gesture lately made by a leader of those classes that he would leave the Hindu

1. And the latter has since been recognized by another Minister, also in the U. P.

fold and become an adherent of some other religious persuasion; perhaps *any* other religious persuasion. It would appear that religion is not a matter of belief but of worldly convenience. However this may be, the point relevant to my argument is that this huge problem of untouchability and the depressed classes has the most disastrous weakening effect on the Hindu community.[1]

Labour

Other recent developments that should be noticed are the organization of labour and the awakening of women. Both are most welcome to every Indian patriot. The former is as yet limited to urban or industrial labour; agricultural labour is in still greater need of organization. There are several public-spirited men to whom credit should be given for helping labour organize itself. I trust it will not be invidious if I single out one name among them as worthy of special mention: I allude to my friend, Mr. N. M. Joshi of the Servants of India Society, Bombay, to whom high praise should be given for the splendid work he has done in the service of labour. It should be acknowledged that the Government of India have been sympathetic and successive members of the Governor-General's Executive Council have on the whole cooperated cordially with the more moderate and responsible leaders of the Labour movement. Among the officers of the Government of India I desire to make particular mention of the valuable services of Mr. A. G. Clow to promote the well-being of the working classes. Nor must praise be withheld from the Labour Commission, most ably presided over by Mr. Whitley, a former Speaker of the House of Commons.

1. I should like in this connection to make honourable and grateful mention of the temple entry proclamation since made by H. H. the Maharaja of Travancore.

I commend to every one a perusal of the reports of the annual sessions of the All India Women's Conference. They are a record of the activities of public-spirited ladies for improvement in the condition of women. The educated women of India are pulsating with a new life. They have made such advance that, if Mahadeo Govind Ranade, the greatest worker in the field of social reform in the latter half of the nineteenth century, were alive today his heart would rejoice. Among much that is depressing and distressing in the situation and the prospect, one may derive hope for the future from the patriotic activities of the women of India. Not the least encouraging circumstance is that almost with one voice they have refused to be dragged into communal controversies.

The women's movement

Let me go back to my chronological record. In the year 1924, when Lord Olivier was the Secretary of State, the Reforms Enquiry Committee was appointed by the Government of India under the chairmanship of Sir Alexander Muddiman, the then Home Member, to enquire into the working of the Montagu-Chelmsford reforms and to make recommendations which could be considered without an amendment of the Act of 1919. The evidence taken by the committee was highly instructive. The spirit in which the bureaucracy frustrated the noble intentions of Mr. Montagu could be read in almost every line of the opinions of provincial governments laid before the committee. Governors in Council constituted themselves the judges of the work of ministers and legislative councils. The latter came in for adverse criticism wherever they did not fall into line with the views of the permanent officials. The tale that ex-ministers had to tell of their respective

The Muddiman Committee

experiences conveyed its own moral. The committee made tepid recommendations. Four of its members—Sir Sivaswamy Aiyer, Sir Tej Bahadur Sapru, Mr. Jinnah and Dr. Paranjpye—made a separate report. Their conclusion was

"that no such transitional system can be devised which can satisfactorily solve the administrative or political difficulties which have been brought to our notice." "To our mind" they added, "the proper question to ask is not whether any alternative transitional system can be devised, but whether the constitution should not be put on a permanent basis with provisions for automatic progress in the future so as to secure stability in the Government and the willing cooperation of the people."

And they urged that a serious attempt should be made at an early date to solve the question. Sir Muhammad Shafi, also a member, signed the majority report ; but on release from office a few weeks later, Sir Muhammad allowed himself to be interviewed and stated that as an official he had been bound by the limits imposed by the scope of the enquiry, but as a nonofficial he agreed with the authors of the Minority Report. Not only was no heed paid to their opinion but even the meagre recommendations of the official section of the committee were not carried into effect.

Exchange

A controversy that raged furiously about this time related to the exchange ratio. Should the value of the rupee in terms of the pound be fixed at 16*d*. or 18*d*. ? Indian opinion was strongly for the former, not unanimously it is true but overwhelmingly. Official opinion was for the higher point. The latter was embodied in a legislative enactment by a narrow majority of the Legislative Assembly. The controversy that surrounds this question is still alive. A large majority of Indians competent to express an opinion has uniformly held that the 18*d*. rupee is disastrous to Indian trade and industries. It today holds that experience has demonstrated this to be so. It is contended that the 18*d*. rupee has aggravated the problem, always serious, of agricultural indebtedness. In 1931 England went off the gold standard, but the Indian rupee was linked to the sterling by an autocratic fiat of the new tory Secretary of State, Sir Samuel Hoare. Since then there has been from India an unprecedented export of gold. While other countries have taken steps to sit tight upon their gold accumulations the spectacle has been presented by India of the unrestricted export of gold, the Government almost gloating over it as a blessing to the country. The whole of the currency and exchange policy of the Government of India since 1893 has been dictated by the City of London through the India Office. The dissent of competent Indians beginning with Dadabhai Naoroji, including R. C. Dutt, D. E. Wacha, G. Subramania Iyer and G. K. Gokhale, and reinforced later by Sir Dadiba Dalal and others has gone for nothing. And we have been presented this year with a new constitution Act in which the British have taken care not to give to the future government and legislature of India the right to decide currency and exchange policy except as the Governor-General may deem to be right. What havoc the policy of the last 42 years has played is sufficiently illustrated by the single case of the sale of reverse councils in 1920, an operation which the *Times of India* described as "organized plunder".

Murder of Swami Shraddhanand

The close of the year 1926 was saddened by a foul tragedy. The revered Swami Shraddhanand was murdered in his own house by a Muslim visitor. The crime was directly due to the Swami's zealous championship of the Hindu cause. Swami Shraddhanand was an ornament of the race. First a practising pleader, Lala (later known as Mahatma) Munshi Ram gave up worldly work and wrote his name in history by the establishment of an educational institution unique in the whole country, the Gurukula of Kangri. A leader of

16

the Arya Samaj, Swamiji (who took the name of Shraddhanand after becoming a Sanyasi) laboured all his life for the elevation of the Hindu community by means of religious and social reform and educational advancement. He was a nationalist to the core and was dragged into active politics by what he had seen of the atrocities of the martial law administration in the Punjab. He acted as chairman of the reception committee of the Congress held at Amritsar in 1919. The murder aroused the greatest indignation in the Hindu community from one end of the country to the other. In Swami Shraddhanand Hindus and India lost a high-souled patriot whose life and services will long remain a treasured possession of the people.

Military policy

Great efforts were made during these years for the liberalization of Britain's military policy in India, carrying with it a substantial reduction of the burdensome military expenditure which has always been not merely excessive but crushing. Mr. Robert Knight, an English journalist in India who earned the gratitude of Indians by his able and vigorous advocacy of their cause, laid down two tests by which to determine the relative share of England and India in the cost of defence. They are the relative capacity and the relative interest of the two countries. Actually, England has uniformly sought to cast upon India as much of the burden as she could decently do, and sometimes more than decency would have permitted. Henry Fawcett, a great friend of India, in his day stigmatized one act of financial injustice as "a masterpiece of melancholy meanness". In truth, the whole chapter has been made up of a series of acts of "melancholy meanness". Commissions and committees have been appointed from time to time ostensibly to give satisfaction to India, but not one of them has resulted in substantial relief to this poor country. Viceroy after Viceroy beginning with Lord Mayo protested against the injustice to India but protested in vain. Lord Northbrook, one of those Viceroys, raised a debate on the subject in the House of Lords in 1893. The Secretary of State admitted the injustice but said that the India Office was not eager to reopen the question because its experience had been that every time this was done the result was the imposition of a fresh burden upon India. Sir Walter Layton, the financial adviser of the Simon Commission, statistically demonstrated that in no other country was so large a part of the revenue absorbed by military expenditure. In a minute written by him a year before the conclusion of the war Sir William Meyer, then Finance Member, a man of uncommon ability who served India faithfully, recorded his opinion that post-war military expenditure in India should not exceed 25 crores per annum. It is notorious that in some years it exceeded double this amount and now it is nearly so. There is no money for social or economic development or educational advancement because of the "home charges" and this military expenditure, parts of that drain of wealth from the country against which Dadabhai Naoroji inveighed all his life. I may here record an observation made to me by Lord Sinha. He said that no Indian knew Englishmen better than he or had a greater admiration for the many splendid traits of their character. But, he added, they should never be trusted where £. *s*. *d*. were involved. It was an Englishman who summed up British character in the phrase " always the purse, often the brain, seldom the heart".

Of the many injuries wrought by foreign rule none has been so grievous as the military policy of Britain in India. In one word it is a policy of distrust. Right up to the year 1917 Indians *as such* were completely excluded from the commissioned ranks of the army. Since the removal in principle of the disability in that year progress in the Indianization of the commissioned ranks of the army has been made at a snail's pace. At the present rate, which Government have shown no disposition to accelerate, the army of India will not be wholly Indianized even after three hundred years. The Government committee known to fame as the Skeen Committee made more or less liberal recommendations but to no effect, presumably because the committee included "a majority of Indian gentlemen", a phrase employed by the Simon Commission probably to justify the rejection of its recommendations. The report of the Defence sub-Committee of the first Round Table Conference did not err on the side of liberality in the recommendations which it embodied, but even its utterly inadequate proposals have not been faithfully carried into effect. A committee was appointed a few months later presided over by Sir Philip Chetwode and it reached such conclusions that the Indian members including such a man as General Rajwade of Gwalior had to dissent from them. I said in an address delivered 15 years ago : "Does England ask for India's trust ? She on her part must trust India. And England's military policy will be the touchstone of her sincerity." I am obliged to say that she has not proved her sincerity. I cannot leave this part of the subject without paying the highest tribute to our honoured countryman, Sir Sivaswamy Aiyer, for the invaluable services he has rendered in this cause with a knowledge, ability, wisdom and devotion all his own.

I must here come back to the subject of constitutional reform. Having rejected the nation-wide demand that the earliest steps should be taken to amend the Government of India Act of 1919 so as to confer responsible government on India the tory Government in England suddenly decided in 1927 to ante-date by two years the statutory commission provided for by that Act. The Secretary of State, Lord

Birkenhead, candidly stated that he should not leave the appointment of the commission to a Labour Government which might come into office. The result was the Simon Commission.

The Simon Commission

The Simon Seven were all Englishmen. It was not only that Indians *qua* Indians were excluded but the reasons given therefor were the most insulting. It was a mere pretext that the Commission must consist of members of Parliament and therefore must necessarily be exclusively British, for at that time there were two Indians in Parliament, Lord Sinha in the House of Lords and Mr. Saklatwala in the House of Commons. The British Government would not include even the former. The stamp of inferiority was fixed on the brow of Indians merely because they were not "God's own Englishmen". In this the official leaders of the Labour party concurred. India's answer was a boycott of the Commission. In this boycott the lead was given by Sir Tej Bahadur Sapru, the supporters of boycott included such men as Sir Sivaswamy Aiyer, and Congressmen and Liberals acted together. The processions of boycotters were answered by police *lathi* charges and the principal victim, as I have said earlier, was Lala Lajpat Rai. The Commission's inquiries aroused little interest in the country and when its belated report was produced in 1930 it amazed Indians by some of its astounding proposals. India was not to have dominion status, she was not to have a responsible central government. The present Legislative Assembly must give place to a body indirectly elected which could be trusted to be more acquiescent in executive decrees. The army of India was to be under the control of his Majesty's Government in England, India however paying for its cost. It is needless to say more upon this portentous document than that Sir Sivaswamy Aiyer of all people dismissed it with the remark that it "should be placed on the scrap-heap".

The Nehru Committee

India did not content herself with the negative answer of boycott to the insult of the Simon Commission. The Congress set up a committee, in which the cooperation of other parties was sought, to draw a scheme of constitution which would answer the requirements and satisfy the aspirations of the country. This committee produced in the middle of 1928 a report known after its president, Mr. Motilal Nehru. The members of the committee included Sir Ali Imam, Sir Tej Bahadur Sapru and Mr. Subhas Chandra Bose. The Nehru Committee Report was accepted by an All Parties' Conference held at Lucknow in the August of that year, under the chairmanship of Dr. Ansari, the President of the Congress. A large section of Muslims, however, rejected the Nehru Committee's scheme of communal representation on the basis of joint electorates. Maulana Mahammad Ali, an ex-president of the Congress, joined in the Muslim communal protest. A National Convention was held in Calcutta in Christmas week of that year. But there, while dominion status as against absolute independence was accepted after a whole day of heated discussion by an overwhelming majority made up mostly of adherents of the Congress, the communal question proved once more the stumbling block and the Convention ended without result.

Lord Irwin's announcement

Lord Irwin, the Viceroy, had been a party to the constitution of an exclusively British statutory commission. But the force of events in India convinced him of the necessity of some step to appease Indian discontent. Honest and God-fearing, Lord Irwin was the most righteous Viceroy after Lord Ripon and he had the courage to press his point of view upon his Majesty's Government in England. It was fortunate that when he went there in the summer of 1929 the Labour Government was in office and the Secretary of State for India was a man so good and true as Mr. Wedgwood Benn. The result of Lord Irwin's mission was the Round Table Conference. He announced it on Oct. 31 of that year in a statement which evoked hearty applause. The Liberal Federation welcomed the announcement

as it authoritatively confirms the view that dominion status for India was what was intended by the Declaration of 1917, as it definitely recognizes that British India and the Indian states should together form a greater united India and as it concedes India's claim to a right to confer on a footing of equality with the British Cabinet on the form of the future constitution for India.

Congress attitude

Every endeavour was made to persuade the leaders of the Congress to cooperate in the work of the Round Table Conference, but they demanded impossibilities as conditions precedent of their participation in the conference and after breaking with the Viceroy, they hastened to Lahore to meet in Congress under the presidentship of Mr. Jawaharlal Nehru and there passed a resolution that India must have complete independence. Soon after the civil disobedience movement was started. The Government met it by a series of repressive ordinances which rained upon India in quick succession. One of them re-enacted the press legislation of 1910 with aggravating features. Some of the other ordinances gave to executive and police officers the most extensive powers free of judicial control. The ordinances did not improve in actual administration. They were administered not with ordinary vigour but with extreme rigour. It has been the traditional duty of Liberals the world over to be jealous of security of person and property, freedom of the press and of association. And although they utterly disapproved of the method of direct action resorted to by the Congress, at a juncture, too, when they could have most usefully cooperated in the work of the Round Table Conference and made it more fruitful, the Liberals of India showed themselves to be fully alive to their duty of standing up for constitutional right and they were as vehement as anybody in the country in the denunciation of the heartless severity of Government repression.

First Round Table Conference

The first Round Table Conference assembled in London in the November of that year (1930). It was opened by his Majesty the King himself and it was presided over by the Prime Minister. It included leading members of the three political parties of England and members of every community and every organization except the Congress. I say members and not representatives for the reason that they were the nominees of the British Government and not the chosen of their countrymen. On the whole they did their best for the cause dear to the heart of every Indian: *On the whole* and *their best*—it should be mentioned that there was a large number of reactionaries and communalists among the Indians selected by the Government. I was convinced then, and have all along thought that the first Conference would have yielded far better results if the Congress had been represented at it. The Conference itself took no decisions and made no recommendations, thanks to the procedure followed by the Premier-chairman, possibly due to insufficient time. The recommendations made by the sub-committees of the Conference left much to be desired but included a number of proposals which, if translated into Act of Parliament, would have carried India far on the road to self-government. But they were not. That within limits that Conference was a success was proved by the almost immediate release of Congress leaders in jail, followed by the conference between the

Viceroy and Mr. Gandhi. This led to conclusions which enabled the Congress to call off civil disobedience and the Government to release all political prisoners. Recriminations soon followed by either party against the other for not observing in the letter and the spirit the conditions of what has come to be known as the Irwin-Gandhi Pact and at one time Mahatma Gandhi gave up on this account his intention of attending the second Round Table Conference. Thanks to Lord Willingdon, the new Viceroy, the difficulties were solved and the Congress was represented at the Conference by the Mahatma himself. Some other leading members of the Congress also attended it in their individual capacity, among them Pandit Madan Mohan Malaviya and Mrs. Sarojini Naidu.

Second Round Table Conference

Mahatma Gandhi made a mistake in constituting himself the sole representative of the Congress. He miscalculated his strength and refused to consider the utility of numbers in a conference. Statesmanship was required in a member of the Conference if he was to pull his weight. In the spring of that year there was an assemblage at Lucknow called the Muslim Nationalist Conference presided over by Sir Ali Imam. It recorded a strong resolution against separate communal electorates. The nationalist Muslims were excluded from the Conference except for Sir Ali Imam, and for reasons best known to himself he remained a more or less silent member. At the second Round Table Conference as at the first the communal question loomed large and efforts made to solve it by consent proved unsuccessful. By this time the Labour party had gone out of office and a Government tory in all but name was installed in Downing Street. The mentality of the new British Government delegation was quite different from that of the previous year. Sir Samuel Hoare succeeded Mr. Wedgwood Benn. It is only necessary to mention the two names for one to conclude that a new attitude was inevitable. The second Conference was altogether more unsatisfactory than the first. The first Conference, when there was a Labour Government with Mr. Wedgwood Benn as Secretary of State, was followed by the release of political prisoners and the abandonment of civil disobedience. The second Conference, when there was a tory yclept National Government with Sir Samuel Hoare as Secretary of State was followed by the resumption of civil disobedience and repression—still more severe than in 1930.

More taxation

In the interval the economic situation deteriorated enormously, the hardest hit being the agriculturists due to a tremendous fall in the prices of primary commodities. Governments everywhere found themselves confronted by very heavy deficits. Their solution was the imposition of new taxes. These were felt the more oppressive as without them people were already in sore straits.* Were not the situation and the consequences so serious one might be amused by the Government's attitude of more taxation as the remedy for every financial difficulty that confronted them. The people being as poor as they are and taxation being so heavy, one would have thought that Government would be impressed by the supreme need of economy—which as the greatest of financial statesmen, Gladstone said, is "itself a source of revenue"—so that funds might be released for beneficial expenditure. But our Government being neither national nor responsible, is neither responsive nor sympathetic and has got into the incurable habit of thinking only in terms of more and still more taxes. So much so, that the following passage from Sydney Smith, written over a hundred years ago to des-

* From here to the end of the quotation is new matter.

cribe taxation in England at that time, may be cited as being apposite at the present day :—

> Taxes upon every article which enters into the mouth, or covers the back, or is placed under the foot—taxes upon everything which is pleasant to see, hear, feel, smell, or taste—taxes upon warmth, light and locomotion—taxes on everything on earth and the waters under the earth, on everything that comes from abroad, or is grown at home—taxes on the raw material—taxes on every fresh value that is added to it by the industry of man—taxes on the sauce which pampers man's appetite, and the drug that restores him to health—on the ermine which decorates the judge, and the rope which hangs the criminal—on the poor man's salt, and the rich man's spice—on the brass nails of the coffin, and the ribands of the bride. At bed or board, couchant or levant, one must pay—the schoolboy whips his taxed top—the beardless youth manages his taxed horse, with a taxed bridle, on a taxed road :—and the dying Englishman, pouring his medicine, which has paid 7 per cent., into a spoon that has paid 15 per cent.—flings himself back upon his chintz bed, which has paid 22 per cent.—and expires in the arms of an apothecary who has paid a licence of a hundred pounds for the privilege of putting him to death. His whole property is then immediately taxed from 2 to 10 per cent. Beside the probate, large fees are demanded for burying him in the chancel ; his virtues are handed down to posterity on taxed marble ; and he is then gathered to his fathers—to be taxed no more.

'No rent' campaign

In the United Provinces, where the system of land tenure is zamindari and not ryotwari as in Madras the Government made almost a fatal delay in the announcement of relief to agriculturists, and when they did announce it, it was found to be hopelessly inadequate. Congressmen, who at heart never approved of the Irwin-Gandhi Pact,—at least one of them is reported to have wept over it,—seized this occasion and started the proposal of a no-rent campaign. The Government of the United Provinces, however, made amends for their dilatoriness soon after the return of Sir Malcolm Hailey from England, and announced substantial concessions both to zamindars and tenants and they went on by successive revisions to make the concessions more generous. But the United Provinces Congress Committee spoiled for a fight and unfortunately succeeded in getting the sanction of the working committee of the Congress. The no-rent campaign was actually started while Mahatma Gandhi was still out of India and when he returned he found himself confronted by the accomplished facts of the no-rent campaign on one side and ordinances on the other. There were ordinances specially for Bengal and the Frontier Province and one separately to deal with the no-rent campaign in the United Provinces. Mahatma Gandhi tried hard to see the Viceroy in the hope of being able to adjust matters. Unfortunately his Excellency declined to have any talk on the Bengal and Frontier ordinances and almost immediately Mahatma Gandhi, Mr. Vallabbhai Patel and others were deported under the same barbaric regulations upon which the Government had relied earlier to arrest and detain people without charge or trial. Mr. Jawaharlal Nehru was arrested when he was on his way to Bombay to meet Mr. Gandhi.

Civil disobedience again

The fat was in the fire and there was a renewed campaign of mass civil disobedience. It was met by swift execution on the part of the Government. They had kept ready any number of ordinances with a view to eventualities and lost no time in promulgating them in breathless succession. It was anticipated that the second campaign would end more quickly than the first. It did not. The discontent in the country was so acute and so widespread, the dissatisfaction with the Government so intense, that unsuspected success attended the call of the Congress and thousands again came forward readily to court imprisonment and suffer the consequences. The Government was relentless, the Congress was unbending. To be a Congressman was virtually to invite imprisonment. Almost every leader was very soon withdrawn from the movement, yet it did not abate. The police excesses this time were at least as bad as in 1930 but no redress was forthcoming; no response to appeals even by unofficial Englishmen for the practice of greater moderation and humanity. No wonder that in the end the movement was crushed. The challenge of the Congress was to the very existence of the British Government. It was not to be expected that the gauntlet would not be picked up by the latter nor must one ever forget how unequally matched the contending parties were. Attempts made in 1930 to bring about an understanding between the Government and the Congress proved signally unsuccessful due in the main to the obduracy of the leaders, although Lord Irwin showed extreme anxiety to find some *modus vivendi*. No attempt succeeded in 1932 either. In the former year the Secretary of State was Mr. Wedgwood Benn while in 1932 he was Sir Samuel Hoare. The latter publicly declared his determination to see the thing to a finish. He was not for any compromise. The movement collapsed by 1933, but it was not formally suspended until the year following.

Communal 'award'

In the August of 1932 was published what was called the Prime Minister's communal award. It was in reality the decision of the British Government. It was grossly unfair to the Hindus, most so to the Hindus of Bengal and the Punjab where they form minorities. One of the provisions which it embodied was separate electorates for the depressed classes. To this Mahatma Gandhi had such objection that he began an interminable fast in Yerrowda jail.

The Poona Pact

The leaders of the community hurried there to prevent a catastrophe and they concluded an agreement with the depressed classes which, while it did not completely do away with separation at one stage, enormously increased the quantum of representation accorded to those classes by the Government's decision. This has hit hard the Hindu community as a whole and nowhere more than in Bengal, where ridiculously excessive representation has been given by the Government to the Europeans at the expense of both Hindus and Muslims and by Hindu leaders assembled at Poona to the depressed classes. The only excuse for this "Poona Pact" was that it became necessary to save Mr. Gandhi's life.

Unity Conference

Following the conclusion of the depressed classes controversy Pandit Madan Mohan Malaviya with his incorrigible optimism which refuses to take note of facts, made haste to hold a Unity Conference at Allahabad. The communities were well represented and the veteran Salem hero, Mr. Vijiaraghavachariar presided over its deliberations. A complete and final agreement was found hard to reach. Many points, however, were amicably settled and the committee of the Conference proceeded to Calcutta there to try to settle the question as it affected Bengal. Two of the points settled were that in the central legislature the Muslims of British India should have 32 per cent. of representation and, secondly, that Sind should be constituted a governor's province subject to a number of safeguards for the Hindu minority and without a subvention from the central revenues. Unfortunately this became public and when the committee of the Conference were in session at Calcutta, Sir Samuel Hoare publicly announced in London that his Majesty's Government had decided that the Muslim representation in the central legislature should be $33\frac{1}{3}$ per cent. and that Sind should be a separate province with a subvention from the central revenues, and (it may be added) without any safeguards for the Hindus. Lo and behold, the committee sitting in Calcutta immediately broke up as one community had no more use for it.

In 1932 another and a very truncated "Round Table Conference" was held in London, but the reactionary spirit reigned supreme. Those members of the first two conferences who were thought to be unaccommodating were rigorously excluded. Sir Samuel Hoare had no use even for a Srinivasa Sastri. The conclusions of this Conference were as they might have been expected to be. I have mentioned one circumstance which illustrates the spirit by which it was informed and also shows why unofficial attempts at Hindu-Muslim unity could not succeed. The foundation of mischief had been laid in the previous year when the so-called Minorities Pact was presented to the Prime Minister. Its inwardness was exposed in a remarkable letter by one who had inside knowledge of all that happened, Sir Edward Benthall. It was appropriately addressed to the "Royalists" of Calcutta and not intended for the eye of the public. But to the confusion of its author it found its way into the press.

Third 'Round Table' Conference'

His Majesty's Government published in March, 1933, in the form of a White Paper their decision on the nature of the new constitution for India. The scheme embodied in the White Paper was so reactionary as to be utterly unacceptable to any section of progressive Indian opinion. It was condemned in downright language by almost all Indian leaders. One could not see in it any family resemblance to many of the recommendations of the Round Table Conference committees. Addressing both houses of the central legislature in July, 1930 Lord Irwin, the Viceroy, said :

The White Paper

> It is the belief of his Majesty's Government that by way of conference it should be possible to reach solutions that both countries and all parties and interests......can honourably accept......Any such agreement at which the conference is able to arrive will form the basis of the proposals which his Majesty's Government will later submit to Parliament. His

Majesty's Government conceive of (the conference) not as a mere meeting for discussion and debate but as a joint assembly of representatives of both countries on whose agreement precise proposals to Parliament may be founded.

Joint Select Committee's Report

Yet the Government took their own line. For all the regard they paid to the opinions of the Indian members of successive Round Table Conferences they might never have convened them. The White Paper scheme was a cruel denial of the most cherished aspirations of the people of this country. It was submitted to examination by a Joint Select Committee of the two houses of Parliament and some Indians were associated with the Committee during the examination of witnesses. They had no part or lot in the Committee's deliberations. Two memoranda were submitted to it, one by all British Indian delegates headed by his Highness the Aga Khan and the other separately by Sir Tej Bahadur Sapru. Their proposals did not err on the side of excess. But they were cast to the winds almost as if they had been the ravings of maniacs, and the majority of the Joint Select Committee made recommendations dotting the i's and crossing the t's of the White Paper except where it was made worse. The most objectionable of the changes for the worse was the abolition of direct representation to the central legislative assembly. This report was condemned in unmeasured accents by every public organization and public man who was not content with communalism run riot and retrogression in the name of reform. It is not to be thought that there can be a scheme so large as this without some good features in it. I admit that there are some such. But our duty is to examine the scheme as a whole and strike a balance of the entries on the credit and the debit side. India's conclusion is that the latter preponderate over the former, certainly in respect of the central government, and that on the whole the so-called reform is not a constitutional advance that should be acclaimed. In this conclusion Congressmen, Liberals and other nationalists see eye to eye with one another.

The new Government of India Act

But the tory Government in England would not listen to Indian opinion. They were concerned almost exclusively with the revolt of the die-hards of their own party and went on making concessions to propitiate them, always at the expense of India. The result is the Government of India Act of the present year. It is India's misfortune that she is so divided by communal and other differences that a truly effective protest cannot be made in a practical form against a great wrong as smaller and more homogeneous communities might have been able to do.

All India Federation is always to be welcomed. A federal constitution for the central government is a step in the right direction. The abolition of the dyarchical governments in provinces must be approved. The large extension of the franchise is the very best feature of the whole scheme. This said, nearly everything that can be said in favour of the new Act has been said. The Federation that will come into being one day will be a confederation *sans* name. Indian ruling princes through their nominees in the federal legislature will be in a position effectually to interfere in matters of exclusive concern to British India, but the latter will not be permitted to say one word with regard to the governance of the states. The princes have to submit to the exercise by the British Government of its undefined rights of paramountcy but are not willing to repose confidence either in their own subjects or in their countrymen of British India. The people of the states will have no more of political rights than they possess at present. In the large majority of the states, as I have already said, they have no rights whatsoever and they will remain unrepresented in the federal legislature. The British Government has retained in its hands through the

Governor-General and the governors of provinces almost every power to make its will and the interests of Britain prevail. Defence is forbidden ground for the new government and legislature. The future Finance Minister will certainly have to perform the duty of raising revenue by imposing taxes, but he will not have the right of determining how the bulk of the revenue so raised shall be spent. He will practically be a cypher. The future government and legislature will be able to do little for the protection of India's trade and industries, because they can only act within the limits set by the British Government from the point of view of British exploiting interests. "Law and order" will doubtless be in the hands of ministers but subject to a special position accorded to the police and to the exercise by governors and the Governor-General of their almost unlimited right to exercise "individual judgment" or to act in their discretion. The all-India services will continue to be under the special care of the Secretary of State. He will recruit them, not the Government of India, and officers of the I. C. S., the I. P., the I. M. S., and other all-India services will retain their privileged position and be able, if so minded, to confound imprudent ministers who may rashly think of controlling them. There will be separate electorates which, there is every reason to fear, will increase communal disunity rather than promote harmony.[1] Then there are the second chambers in the majority of provinces. The Punjab

---

[1] In an article on "self-rule for India" contributed to an American publication, "Current History" for October, 1935, Mr. H. B. Lees-Smith, who was a member of the last Labour Government, writes as follows :—

"The age-long antagonism between Hindu and Muslim thus becomes stereotyped in the electoral system, and the healthy growth of parties representing divergent economic and social policies is rendered almost impossible. The mobile body of political opinion which, by throwing itself against a party with an extravagant or obsolete policy, keeps democracy on an even keel will try in vain to make headway against the fixed number of members

is denied the blessing because I suppose the majority there is Muslim. Lord Russell of Killowen described the British House of Lords as "the ancient enemy of every righteous cause". Our mimic House of Lords in Delhi and Simla has, during the fifteen years of its existence, earned a title to a similar distinction. The coming provincial second chambers may not do less. I fear that they will block progressive agrarian legislation, and thereby facilitate the task of the advocates of direct action. Lastly, India loses Burma and Aden. If there is an Indian who can enthuse over this scheme of reform I confess I am not he, and if I should find him I will not envy him.

Terrorism in Bengal

Terrorism in Bengal, which made its first appearance during the anti-partition agitation nearly 28 years ago, is not yet a thing of the past. The Government have been unsparing in their endeavour to eradicate it as any government is bound to be, but they have not succeeded or their success is very partial. The mistake they have made is to rely almost wholly on repression. Legislative and administrative repression has been practised with such vigour that there is reason to fear that the innocent

in the communal electorates. The principle of communal electorates having once been accepted for Muslims, it was extended to the Sikhs, the Indian Christians, the depressed classes, the Anglo-Indians, the Europeans, women, the commercial interests, labour and the landlords."

"The cumulative result of giving a privileged position to Muslims, Sikhs, the depressed classes, the princes and the rest has finally come back like a boomerang upon the Hindu nationalist leaders. Their followers are left on the general register, which now is represented by less than one-third of the members of the federal legislature. Even if the Nationalists sweep the whole register, they remain permanently a minority. Gandhi and Congress have won parliamentary government for India, but in doing so they have had to concede to implacable minorities of their own people a series of compromises which have put them in chains for generations to come."

have suffered along with the guilty. Sometimes the method and manner of repression has been a nuisance to law-abiding people. Where the innocent were seized bitterness naturally followed. It should have been the Government's aim to enlist public sympathy for their measures whose motive and object is unexceptionable. Nobody wants terrorism to continue. I suspect that even among the terrorists themselves there must be not a few who would gladly give up their nefarious activities and live by honourable means if they could. But the vice of the bureaucracy to think too much of its own capacity has prevailed and the public are left mere lookers-on of measures at least some of which are excessive and are administered with little regard for human feelings. They would fain influence Government's policy if they could, but no heed is paid to their counsel. The bureaucracy have never learnt the lesson of history that opinion is the best support of law and that to alienate opinion is not a sign of wisdom in government. One more point is that the Government have shown very insufficient recognition of a fact patent to every observer endowed with common sense, that the struggle for existence is at the root of the terrorist movement as of political distempers in general. The miserable plight of the educated youth of Bengal was emphasized by an official committee—the Bengal District Administration Committee presided over by Sir Verney Lovett, K.C.S.I., I.C.S.—and they proposed a number of ameliorative measures. There is little evidence that the Government of Bengal have made an earnest effort to carry into effect any important recommendation of the committee. Only during the last few weeks has there been a glimmer of hope that at long last they have become alive to the necessity of some constructive work. Whether their proposals will bear fruit time will show. I see light in an unexpected place. Into the uncongenial pages of the Bengal Administration Report of 1934 has crept the following sentence which one would have expected to find in the columns of nationalist newspapers : "Terrorism has not yet been eradicated from Bengal and never will be merely by special legislation." May it be hoped that this will be engraven on the heart of every Governor of Bengal ? May it be further hoped that its larger application will be borne in mind by all Viceroys and Governors ?

Unemployment

Unemployment is not an evil limited to Bengal. In western countries the extensive unemployment of the labouring classes has become a political problem of the first magnitude. In India there is permanent unemployment among the agricultural masses for several months every year. Imports of foreign goods and the development of industries in India have both increased rural unemployment by depriving the agriculturists of their subsidiary occupations. But while the existence of the problem has been recognized, it has only been met with a sigh and dismissed without a shudder. Unemployment among the educated classes has, however, become increasingly rife and assumed the dimensions of a grave national problem. There have been sporadic attempts to find some solution for it, but so far without success. Two unemployment committees are at present sitting, one in the United Provinces and the other in Bihar. The former has of the advantage of the chairmanship of Sir Tej Bahadur Sapru, who to my knowledge has bestowed continuous and conscientious labour and thought upon the enquiry. The report of his committee is expected to be in the hands of the public in a few weeks from now, but the result will depend in the main upon Government action. [1] One thing is certain. If

1. The report has since been published It embodies the most comprehensive treatment of the subject yet made anywhere in India, and

Government are unable or unwilling to find money to expend upon constructive measures no number of committees can help. Mahatma Gandhi's Village Industries Aid Association has spurred the Government to some action for rural development. [2] The result is in the future.

The Press

Journalism during this period has sustained its progress notwithstanding more than ordinary difficulties placed in its way by Government policy. In the Madras presidency there is the *Andhra Patrika*, for which the people are indebted to the philanthropy and patriotism of a gentleman who must be honoured wherever good work is valued—Mr. K. Nageswara Rao. It has been a great educator of the Andhra population as the *Swadesa Mitran* has been of the Tamil. The *Hindu* has continued to achieve remarkable success and maintained its position as the foremost of Indian papers. After Mr. Kasturiranga Iyengar it had a very able editor in Mr. A. Rangaswami Iyengar, a careful student of constitutional as well as financial problems. His premature death is a great loss both to journalism and to public life in India. *Justice* has been conducted in the interests of the party that bears that name. Two other daily papers in Madras are *Swarajya* and the *Indian Express*.—Mr. Jehangir Petit of Bombay spent lakhs of rupees on the *Indian Daily Mail*, but it did not flourish. The *Dnyan Prakash* of Poona, a Marathi daily paper taken over by Mr. Gokhale on behalf of the Servants of India Society, has continued to do good work. The *Servant of India* is an English weekly paper conducted

I am glad to acknowledge that within the limits of their financial capacity the United Provinces Government have been doing their best to give effect to the Committee's recommendations. The Government of India, too, under Lord Linlithgow's leadership, have been giving serious consideration to the report.

2. The present Viceroy is specially interested in this subject.

by the Society. Its first editor was Mr. Srinivasa Sastri himself. After him Messrs. S. G. Vaze and P. Kodanda Rao, both members of the Society, have been doing excellent public service through its columns. Mr. Horniman has got back to Indian journalism and now edits the *Bombay Sentinel*.—In Bengal Surendranath Banerjea's *Bengalee* has come to an end as, earlier still both the *Hindoo Patriot* and the *Indian Mirror* did. But the *Amrita Bazar Patrika* retains its position of primacy. It has lost during this period its greatest editor, Babu Motilal Ghosh, as the *Hindu* lost Messrs. Kasturiranga and Rangaswami Iyengar. Two other papers, both of the Congress school, were started during this period, *Forward* and *Advance*.[1] The *Ananda Bazar Patrika*, a Bengali newspaper, first started by the brothers Sisir Kumar and Motilal Ghosh, has passed into other hands and can now boast of the largest circulation of any newspaper in India.—Lala Lajpat Rai started at Lahore the *Bande Mataram* in Urdu and the *People* in English. The latter is the organ of the Servants of the People Society, also founded by him.—Delhi has now two nationalist papers in the *Hindustan Times* (for which the country is indebted to Lala Lajpat Rai, Pandit Madan Mohan Malaviya and Mr. Ghanshyam Das Birla) and the *National Call*.—Newspapers in Bihar have never had an easy time of it owing to the geographical situation of Patna. There are in that city two nationalist papers—the *Searchlight* (Congress) and the *Indian Nation* (owned by the Maharajadhiraj of Darbhanga).—The Central Provinces have now the *Daily News* and a paper owned by the Servants of India Society, the *Hitavada*.—Two prominent journalists of this period who deserve honourable mention for good work done are Babu Kalinath Roy, the veteran editor of the *Tribune* of Lahore, and Mr. S. A. Brelvi,

1. The *Hindusthan Standard* is the latest of Congress English dailies in Calcutta.

editor of the *Bombay Chronicle*.—In this very period Mahatma Gandhi too has been a journalist, first through his *Young India* in English and *Navajivan* in Gujarati and now *through* the *Harijan*. Unique as a politician, he is equally unique as a journalist. He does not allow a single advertisement to be inserted in any of his papers. His writings are in simple English of Biblical purity.

Personalities

Mahatma Gandhi

Among the public men of this period the first place goes, naturally and necessarily, to Mahatma Gandhi, the rare and unique personality, with whom there is none to compare. No public man before him or during his time has acquired the same ascendancy over the public mind as he has done. Mr. Gokhale drew the following word picture of him in his speech at the Lahore Congress of 1909 :—

> After the immortal part which Mr. Gandhi has played in this affair (the South Africa Indians' struggle) I must say it will not be possible for any Indian at any time here or in any other assembly of Indians to mention his name without deep emotion and pride. It is one of the privileges of my life that I know Mr. Gandhi intimately ; and I can tell you that a purer, a nobler, a braver and a more exalted spirit has never moved on this earth. Mr. Gandhi is one of those men, who, living an austerely simple life themselves and devoted to all the highest principles of life, to their fellow-beings and to truth and justice, touch the eyes of their weaker brethren as with magic and give them a new vision. He is a man who may be well described as a man among men, a hero among heroes, a patriot amongst patriots, and we may well say that in him Indian humanity at the present time has really reached its high watermark.

There are in Mr. Gandhi many qualities which entitle him to the honorific which his countrymen have bestowed upon him. Truly is he a Mahatma. In his day he was a great success at the bar. But even then I had it from himself that if at any stage of a case he had reason to think that his client had not instructed him truthfully he threw up the brief and returned the fee. Whatever he had saved as the result of years of practice at the bar he gave away to his countrymen in South Africa. He had no use for money. In fact he has contempt for money except where it is required for the service of his countrymen. To the quality of fear he is a complete stranger. I do not know another man who has banished the very thought of fear completely from his life as the Mahatma has done. He is deeply spiritual, while of moral virtues what has he not? He has mastered and practised the truth given to humanity by Siva himself :

ममेति परमंदुःखं नममेति परं सुखम् ।

He is not a formal Sanyasi, but there is no greater Sanyasi than he in the world, for in his person he has realized the ideal held up by Sri Krishna :

ज्ञेयस्स नित्य सन्यासी योनद्वेष्टि न कांक्षति ।
निर्द्वन्द्वोहि महाबाहो सुखंबन्धात् प्रमुच्यते ॥

He has no desire and no hate. Truly is he a जीवनमुक्त. He is like Dadabhai Naoroji in his unceasing attack on the system of government established in this country but without personal ill-will against a single individual called upon to administer that system :

आत्मवत्सर्वभूतानि यः पश्यति स पश्यति ।

So indeed does Mahatma Gandhi. Take him all in all, no Indian need hesitate to look upon this great soul as the greatest man on earth today. That in this decadent age Providence should have blessed India with a son like Mahatma Gandhi is proof to those who have Faith that notwithstanding all that looks so unpromising at the moment, God wills that this holy land of the Munis and Rishis shall again have a future worthy of her ancient glory. Gandhi and Tagore between them have made the India even of today respected throughout the civilized world.

All this conceded, what is Mr. Gandhi as a politician? It is not given to man to be perfect or infallible. Possibly even divine incarnations are not when they come to live in this world in human form. Infallibility and Perfection are attributes of the Divine. I believe with Lord Acton that absolute devotion to mortal man ought not to exist, and with Mr. Bertrand Russell that it is dangerous to regard any one man as infallible—I will add, Mr. Gandhi not excepted. Therefore no one need fear that he detracts from the respect that is Mahatma Gandhi's due if he thinks that he has his limitations. Whether he would have been a greater man if he had not taken to politics need not be speculated upon. My study of Mr. Gandhi has led me to the conclusion that while he is the greatest man among all who have served India in the political sphere during the last hundred years, he certainly is not one of the wisest political leaders the country has had. When his numerous inconsistencies and serious mistakes as a political leader are considered without partiality or prejudice, I at any rate cannot resist the conclusion that whatever may be the future effects of his policy it has done positive harm in the present. Mr. J. A. Spender has written of Disraeli's "perennial pose of being a man of mystery and destiny". If we eliminate "pose" the description fits Mahatma Gandhi admirably. The misfortune is that politics is not exactly the sphere for such a man. India being admittedly unfit for organized physical resistance of authority—I leave on one side the ethics of non-violence as a political method—I hold that there is no alternative to constitutional agitation open to us at present. I do not swear by it as I would by a religious creed. To me the question is wholly one of methods appropriate in a given situation. Mahatma Gandhi has asked whether there is a single instance in history of a subject nation regaining its lost liberty by the pursuit of the constitutional method. May I ask him in return whether he can furnish a solitary instance of its being achieved by methods such as his ? It is not the concern of politicians what a distant future may bring forth and what may have to be done then. Let us deal with the situation as it is before us, the politicians of the future may be left to grapple with their own problems. We have to deal with time, not with eternity. We are concerned with today and tomorrow, not with what may happen during the time of our sons and grandsons. If Mahatma Gandhi had not come forward with his nostrum of non-cooperation just on the eve of the introduction of the present reforms, the whole of politics during the last fifteen years would very likely have been different. Indian nationalists would have remained a united body of men and would have in office, in legislatures and in outside public life brought to bear upon the British Government a pressure the result of which would in my opinion have been very different from what has actually been the consequence of the divisions in public life brought to a head and rendered inevitable by Mr. Gandhi's policy. His non-violent non-cooperation is just one of those double negatives, if there be any other, which do not make an affirmative. In passive resistance the Mahatma lays equal stress upon both words of the phrase. But it is the substantive that has appealed to not a few of his followers and not the limiting adjective. His civil disobedience campaign has wrought the greatest misery in thousands of families. And so much sacrifice and suffering has led—whither ? Not to Swaraj, but back to the councils ! Mahatma Gandhi has rightly preached, as he himself has practised all his life, अहिंस, than which there is no greater धर्म. But the political methods which he has inculcated have brought upon those who have followed him nothing but हिंस. The party against which his policy has been directed is just the party which has taken the utmost advantage of the situation created by him and deprived the whole people of a modicum of such civil liberties as they enjoyed before. Who but a miracle-man—and this is not the age of miracles if ever there was—would have promised Swaraj in twelve months ? The very slave mentality which he condemned led thousands of people to believe in this as if they were so many children. If it is my belief that Mahatma Gandhi is not only the greatest Indian but the greatest of men of today, not less strong is my conviction that in politics he has committed grave blunders which have produced immense mischief. One thing, however, there is to be said in his favour as a politician. As a result of his preaching there has been an awakening among the masses, a widely diffused national consciousness, a readiness to sacrifice and suffer, to bear and brave for which the country would have had to wait longer if there had been no Gandhi. It need not be doubted that this national awakening will prove in future to be an asset of great value. For this no honest critic of Mr. Gandhi's politics will hesitate to give him the greatest credit. Politics is ephemeral. Character lives. When all controversies of the day are forgotten the name and character of Mohandas Karamchand Gandhi will live. He is a living sermon on the noblest and the most difficult of virtues and in India's history his name and life will shine in glittering characters of gold. To us all it must be a source of infinite pride that we are privileged to be the countrymen of this rare man.

OTHER PUBLIC MEN

Sir Sivaswamy Aiyer

Among the public men of this period I cannot give a higher place to any one, always excepting Mahatma Gandhi and Pandit Madan Mohan Malaviya, than to Sir P. S. Sivaswamy Aiyer. His character, his ability, his learning, his wide and accurate knowledge and his uncommon power of judgment are national assets which would have been valued and honoured in any country in the world. A sounder thinker there is not in our midst.

Mr. Srinivasa Sastri

The rt. hon. V. S. Srinivasa Sastri, Mr. Gokhale's successor in the Servants of India Society, has acquired an international reputation. Scholar and educationist, he has won admiration by his remarkable powers of oratory. Honest aud unselfish, the purity of his patriotism is recognized even by those who most differ from him.

There is another gentleman of the same political persuasion who has done great good work during this period as he did in earlier years. Sir M. Ramachandra Rao[1] never undertakes a task to the execution of which he does not bring conscientious thoroughness. He is the greatest master of detail that I know at the present day.—There is then Sir C. P. Ramaswami Aiyer, a man whose uncommon ability attracted the attention of Mr. Montagu.—Mr. G. A. Natesan has distinguished himself both as a journalist and as a public man.—Among Congress leaders in Madras I would give the first place to Mr. C. Rajagopalachari.—In sheer intellect Mr. S. Srinivasa Iyengar was the first of Madras Congressmen of the last decade. If in him steadiness had been joined to brilliance Mr. Srinivasa Iyengar could have done much for the country.—Mr. Konda Venkatappaiya Pantulu is a brave and selfless patriot who is rightly given almost the first place among the public men of the Andhra districts.

Mrs. Sarojini Naidu

Mrs. Sarojini Naidu, Bengali by birth and Deccani by marriage, is a resident of Bombay for purposes of public work. A poet of acknowledged eminence, she has chosen

[1]Sir M. Ramachandra Rao has since passed away.

to give to politics what was meant for poetry and has attained such success as to have become a president of the Congress. She has an engaging personality and her command of English is wonderful. Easily one of the best public speakers in the India of today, she excels still more in conversation. Among living Indians she is the most brilliant conversationalist that I know.

Mr. Jinnah

Mr. Mohammad Ali Jinnah is the acutest of debaters. Fearlessness is a quality that never fails him. I do not suppose that there is any man, whatever his position, before whom Mr. Jinnah has ever hesitated to say the thing he wanted in language not merely plain but blunt. If latterly he has figured less as a nationalist than as a communalist we can but deplore the change as a misfortune of the country.

Dr. Paranjpye

Dr. R. P. Paranjpye is one of the most upright men in public life. There is no make-believe about him. His address as President of the Liberal Federation at Lucknow in December, 1924, was criticized by some friends for inopportune plain speaking against the policy and the leaders of the Congress. His defence was interesting as an expression of the man's character, and is worth quoting. He said:

> I have recently been occasionally charged with being blunt, and frankly I must say that I have always been a blunt man. I have been a teacher all my life and a teacher of (mathematics)........It is not possible for a teacher of mathematics to use vague language. The duty of a teacher of mathematics, above all things, is to be absolutely clear, and I cannot shake off the habits of a lifetime......We have seen very often in our country that we have tried to invent formulæ on which to secure an agreement for the moment and spend the rest of the year in trying to interpret those formulæ, each in his own way. Well, I don't believe in that. I would rather like plain straightforward talk.

It may be mentioned that Dr. Rabindranath Tagore has expressed the same disbelief in such formulæ. The two men who have most influenced Dr. Paranjpye's public life were his teacher, Mr. Gokhale, and his kinsman, Mr. Karve, the honoured founder of the Indian Women's University.

Mr. Vithalbhai Patel was a brave soldier in the struggle for freedom. His younger brother; Mr. Vallabbhai Patel, known as Sardar for his services to the peasantry of Gujarat, is believed to be Mahatma Gandhi's right-hand man.—Mr. N. C. Kelkar is a surviving veteran of the Tilak school.—Mr. M. R. Jayakar came into prominence first as a member of the Home Rule League and next as a non-cooperator. Then he became a "responsive cooperationist". His present political opinions are far more moderate than those of the Liberal party for which he has had never any use. His ability and eloquence are rightly admired.—His Highness the Aga Khan is a statesman who would have been accepted as an all-India leader if unfortunately he had not chosen to give to one community what should have been given to the nation.

C. R. Das

The leading public man of Bengal was Chitta Ranjan Das. He was like Sir George Jessel, who said of himself : "I may be right, I may be wrong, but I have no doubts." Sacrifice was nothing to him ; to do the thing he willed was everything. The thing must be done at any cost by any means. During the few years which was all that was vouchsafed to him of active public life, he was a power to be reckoned with and he dominated Bengal politics as no one else has since been able to do.

The late Mr. J. M. Sen-Gupta and Mr. Subhas Chandra Bose among Congressmen, and the late Sir Provash Mitter and Mr. J. N. Basu, Liberal leaders, are other Bengal public men who deserve to be mentioned.—There is one more name. Sir Abdur Rahim, whose Minority Report as a member of the Royal Commission on Superior Civil

Services known as the Islington Commission was a much admired political document marked by equal ability and patriotism, has been taking a prominent part in affairs. How one could wish that he were less of a Muslim and more of an Indian.

Motilal Nehru

The greatest Congress leader of this period in the United Provinces was Mr. Motilal Nehru. During the major part of his life he was the greatest admirer of the British character and British ways of living. He only came into public life at the age of 46 as president of the first United Provinces Conference. Three years later he went into the Legislative Council. But the first time he took seriously to politics was not before 1917 when he was already 56 years old. Mr. Motilal Nehru held very moderate opinions until that year. Once, however, he gave up his earlier policy, he travelled fast and travelled far in the direction of extremism. And among the Congress leaders of the Gandhian period his place after the Mahatma was by the side of C. R. Das. Intellectually superior to either of them, Mr. Motilal Nehru was the brain of the Congress during the ten years which preceded his death in 1931. And during this period he too did not flinch from any sacrifice including what must have been particularly irksome to a man who lived as he had done, life in jail. He combined the habit of methodical work with keen intellectual power and a one-pointed purpose. The United Provinces and India are the poorer for his death.

Sir Tej Bahadur Sapru

Sir Tej Bahadur Sapru is of a different type. He joined the bar after a brilliant academic career and has attained the first place in the Allahabad High Court. He has been interested in public questions since his college days. He joined public life while he was still a junior member of the bar. He distinguished himself as a politician both in opposition and in office. By dint of his talents he has acquired a high reputation in England where some of the leading statesmen are his friends and admirers. He has always done work of distinction. There have of late been differences of opinion between him and his old colleagues in the party of which he was one of the most prominent leaders, but no differences can cast into the shade his brilliant ability and his valuable services. He is a true friend and has a generous heart and many endearing personal qualities

Mr. Kunzru

I have referred to Pandit Hirday Nath Kunzru as Pandit Ajodhya Nath's son. He is a patriot every inch of him. He devotes the whole of his time, and every day of the year, to the country's work in the spheres of politics, education and social service. A better informed man there is not in the whole country in any party or community. And with knowledge wide and varied are combined a powerful brain and untiring industry. His character is the highest.

Mr. J. Nehru

Mr. Motilal Nehru has given to the country his son, Mr. Jawaharlal Nehru. Educated in England, he came out as a member of the English bar but a lawyer's work was never congenial to him. He was not slow to take to public life, and once there, there is nothing else for which he has cared. Clear in thought and in language, extreme in opinion, determined in action, reckless of consequence, it has been the lot of Mr. Jawaharlal, who might have lived a life of ease and luxury, actually to lead a life of hardship for the sake and in the service of the Motherland. Those who disagree with him admire him equally with his supporters.

One other public man of the United Provinces who deserves honourable mention is Babu Purushottam Das

Tandon. A poor man, he yet gave up his practice and has for years devoted himself solely to public work. He is a brave man and true, to whom sacrifice and suffering have become native, as it were.

Babu Rajendra Prasad

Babu Rajendra Prasad, the President of the Congress, is a man respected by all for his exceeding goodness, complete honesty and unselfish public spirit.—Another public man of Bihar who should be mentioned is Mr. Sachchidananda Sinha, a former Congressman who is now a non-party nationalist. Lawyer, journalist, politician, speaker and debater, Mr. Sachchidananda Sinha has been in public life for nearly forty years and served his province and country well.

Mr. S. Sinha

The distinguished brothers Ali Imam and Hasan Imam died during this period. They did good work in their day.—Two other Congress leaders worthy of mention are Dr. Ansari and Maulana Abul Kalam Azad, both of them ex-presidents of the Congress. The latter is a charming speaker in Urdu.—Sir Moropant Joshi in the Central Provinces is a Liberal leader. He has been in public life for about 48 years. Like other Liberals he was a Congressmen until 1918.—It is rather difficult to place the Ali brothers. Mr. Mohamad Ali was more talented. Maulana Shaukat Ali has perhaps a stronger personality.—Sir Muhammad Shafi was the most prominent public man of the Punjab.

Rabindra Nath Tagore

I have left to the last—because he is not in political life—a son of Bengal whom all India claims and who shares with Mahatma Gandhi a world-reputation. Need I say that I refer to Rabindranath Tagore, the great poet and the prophet of Indian nationalism? I did not see a book-stall at railway stations in England, France, Germany or Belgium where the works of Tagore in the languages of the respective countries are not stocked, A Norwegian gentleman with whom I happend to go from Paris to Versailles told me that Tagore's name was a household word in Norway and that he himself had read translations in his mother-tongue of all his important works. He remarked to me that the people of India must be the best educated in the world. When I told him that illiteracy was the badge of the tribe in our country he exclaimed in wonder, "What, the countrymen of Tagore to be illiterate! Incredible!" Deep must be our gratitude to Providence for giving us such fellow-countrymen as Gandhi and Tagore.

CHAPTER V

CONCLUSION

I here bring to a close the survey I have attempted of the vicissitudes of Indian politics and of the growth of public life in India including the development of ideas and institutions during the 78 years that have elapsed since the Mutiny. What are the conclusions to which India's political history of this period leads? The idea of progress is firmly implanted in the mind of educated India as a whole. Systematic efforts have been made throughout this period by a large number of public-spirited men to achieve political progress. Besides the amelioration of the condition of the people, the aim of the Indian patriot has been to win for the Motherland that which is more precious than anything else, freedom under Swaraj. Without this the honour of the Motherland will not be satisfied. Remember Lord Rosebery's definition of patriotism as "the self-respect of race". Was the effort well-planned? Has the plan been intelligently executed? What success has attended the work done with the right motive and at no little sacrifice? There are more criteria than one by which the position has to be judged. Have public men by their work been able to infuse public spirit into ever increasing numbers of their countrymen? What success have they achieved in obtaining redress of grievances and how far are they from the goal which they have set before themselves? Are they any nearer to it today than before all this work was started? In answering these questions one may derive satisfaction from all that has been accomplished. Equally may one feel disappointed that the ground to be traversed after more

Satisfaction and disappointment

than three-quarters of a century is still so vast and perhaps so much more difficult than that which has been covered. Individual temperament would account for the varying estimates of results which different men might be disposed to make. I remember in 1894 Mr. Ranade, in an address at Madras expressed satisfaction that so much work had been done in the furtherance of social reform. On the same occasion the chairman of the meeting, Dr. (afterwards Sir Ramkrishna) Bhandarkar came to a decidedly unfavourable conclusion on the basis of the same facts and he felt a sense of acute disappointment at the smallness of the result that had been achieved. To me it appears that a correct conclusion can only be drawn if all points of view are kept in mind. One definition of statesmanship is that it is "a many-sided point of view". Recognition of achievements should not blind one to failures. Nor should the magnitude of the task that lies ahead dispose one in a mood of exaggerated pessimism to belittle all that has been accomplished. Optimism and pessimism are both question-begging epithets. There are people so incurably optimistic that they would shut their eyes to facts and, as John Morley said, call it fine weather when it is raining cats and dogs; at the other end are men who would condemn the sun because astronomers say that there are spots on it. The correct attitude is what Mr. Ranade described as "cautious meliorism".

Two questions

Two main questions here arise. What progress have the people made in the organization of public life and the diffusion of public spirit? What action has Government taken to transform itself from an autocratic or bureaucratic and irresponsible into a constitutional, that is, representative and responsible government? The question is, has progress been made with reforms in the system of administration, urged and called for in the interests of the people? Have economic conditions improved or deteriorated? Has education been widely diffused among the people? Have social reforms been carried out with the double object of increasing social efficiency and promoting national unity?

Public life

The first question is the easiest to answer. Such progress has been made in the organization of public life and the diffusion of public spirit among the people that conditions today may be said to bear no comparison with those in which our earliest public men had to do their work. At that time there was no organization worth mentioning. Public spirit was limited to a few individuals here and there. All honour to them that, undismayed by conditions almost deterrent, they did their work so well that on the fundations they laid truly and firmly, a vast structure has been raised of which Indians have no reason to feel ashamed. First isolated workers; next local associations; thirdly, provinicial organizations, and lastly, all-India organizations. Of the last the greatest as it is the oldest is unquestionably the Indian National Congress. Addressing the Congress of 1891 at Nagpur Mr. Hume rejoiced that they had reached its seventh session. The Congress was threatened with a crisis after its first twenty years and actually broke up amid scenes of violence when it assembled in its twenty-second session. It was, however, reconstituted without loss of time. It went into other hands and changed its policy a decade later. Of the founders of the Congress but one[1] is now living, and of its earliest members there are a very few still with us. Many old Congressmen have had to give up their adherence to the institution in which they were

---

1 Sir Dinshaw Wacha. He too is no more.

reared only because of their allegiance to the principles and policy of that very institution. A month more, and the Congress will be celebrating its golden jubilee. In the original sense of the term it can be affirmed that all Indian nationalists are Congressmen; although, due to fundamental changes made in the institution many of them are not and cannot be members of the Congress. The present state of public life in the country is the greatest triumph of the fathers of Indian nationalism. The country is full of agitation, which is only another name for life. Life is hope, effort is hope. And all work done with unselfish motive and sanctified by sacrifice is bound to succeed in the long run, however long the run may be, in the dispensation of the All Good.

The attitude of Congressmen of the present day towards those with whom they disagree leads me to cite the following comparison made by Mr. J. A. Spender between Labour and other political parties in England :—

Congress and other parties

> The older parties cultivated a certain tolerance towards each other; in their easier moments they admitted each other's merits and even conceived it possible that they themselves might be mistaken; Labour would have none of this weakness. It was like the Catholic church—dogmatic, exclusive, Papal—demanding the entire allegiance of its members, absolutely forbidding communion with inferior sects, contemplating always its own infallibility. It might have a difficulty in deciding what its dectrine was but it was at least agreed that there could be no other.

Mr. Bertrand Russell says :

> When conscious activity is wholly concentrated on some one definite purpose the ultimate result for most people is lack of balance accompanied by some form of nervous disorder.
>
> Perhaps there is in the world much too much readiness not only for action without adequate previous reflexion but also for some sort of action on occasions on which wisdom would counsel inaction......Hamlet is held up as an awful warning against thought without action, but no one holds up Othello as a warning against action without thought....For my part I think action is best when it emerges from a profound apprehension of the Universe

and human destiny, not from some wildly passionate impulse of romantic but disproportioned self-assertion....The world at present is full of angry self-centered groups each incapable of viewing human life as a whole, each willing to destroy civilization rather than yielding an inch.

Both private and public misfortune can only be mastered by a process in which will and intelligence interact: the part of will is to refuse to shirk the evil or accept an unreal solution, while the part of intelligence is to understand it, to find a cure if it is curable, and if not, to make it bearable by seeing it in its relations, accepting it as unavoidable and remembering what lies outside it in other regions for ages and the abysses of inter-stellar space.

It is from large perceptions combined with impersonal emotion that wisdom most readily springs.

Obviously a system which demands exceptional qualities of human beings will only be successful in exceptional cases. The badness of such a system is not disproved by the existence of rare instances in which its evils do not appear.

The impatience of the ultra-radicals of today with those of their compatriots whom the consideration of patriotism counsels not to go too fast or too far is unjustified, short-sighted and thoughtless. They question the very motives of public men whose judgment leads them to vote in favour of the constitutional as distinguished from direct action, regardless of the duration, the amount and the quality of their work for the Motherland. They speak and write as if it had all been cimmerian darkness before the day of Mahatma Gandhi; as if he had evolved order out of chaos, something out of nothing, life out of death. A meagre acquaintance with all that went before would suffice to rule this opinion out of court as ignorant if not childish. The present has grown out of the past and would not have been possible without the past. If there had been no Hume or Dadabhai Naoroji there would have been no Congress. Mahatma Gandhi found a ready-made national organization into which he could jump and which he could easily manipulate according to his ideas as the situation favoured him. It was not a case of "let there be light and there was light". If there had been no Ranade and Mehta, no Surendranath Banerjea and Tilak, no

Gokhale and Malaviya, there would have been no Congress for Mr. Gandhi to seize hold of. It is necessary for public men to cultivate a historical sense. It the typical Congressman of today bestowed upon a study of the past a fraction of the energy he expends on the vilification of those who insist upon thinking for themselves in preference to uncritical approval of every changing opinion of the Mahatma there would be less of wrong history, incorrect facts, illogical reasoning and unsound conclusions as well as of ingratitude to our forbears, but for whom things today would be far worse than they are. The homely saying taught to us at school as an example of bad grammar embodies a truth which deserves to be remembered better than it is :

> We call our fathers fools, so wise we grow,
> No doubt our wiser sons will call us so.

Congress unwisdom

Already there are signs that a left wing inside the Congress is growing increasingly impatient and suspicious of the main body. Congress socialists threaten to give no rest or peace to their fellow-Congressmen whom they suspect to be bourgeois in their leanings and interests. What we see today of the former is the small cloud which now is no bigger than a man's hand but which threatens to envelope the whole sky. Unconsidered talk on the abolition of ruling princes and landed magnates can but have the effect of alarming the propertied classes and alienating them from the national movement, just as the talk of the repudiation of the public debt of India has produced suspicion in the British mind and led to at least some of the many "safeguards" in the new Government of India Act. To one who is not in the present Congress it appears to be the veriest commonsense that at the present stage all effort should be concentrated on the winning of Swaraj and the negation of sense to divide the country into warring camps by the adumbration of policies and programmes which, whatever their merit, cannot be carried into effect during the present regime but divide public men to the advantage of the agency which now has the power in its hands and which, humanly enough, it will not part with for as long as it can help. Our first task is to obtain a transfer of power from the hands of non-Indians. How that power is to be distributed among the various elements of our composite nation and what use is to be made of it, are obviously questions for decision after it has been obtained.

These, however, are views which are set down as 'reformist' if not reactionary and scarcely a thought is given to them by the more virile section of the public men of today. No one who has eyes to see, ears to hear and a mind to reflect is under a delusion that the opinions of men of my way of thinking are popular. Frankly they are not. A mere count of heads at any public gathering will show that these opinions are not shared by the majority of people who take an interest in politics. But then the majority of those heads are not instructed heads.

Basis of majority rule

His Holiness Sri Sankaracharya of Sringeri—one of the most extraordinary men I have so far been fortunate enough to meet, if I may say so without presumption—said to some of us last month when we had the privilege of his *darshan* that majority rule implied the competence of the majority to form a judgment. *Vox populi vox Dei* is a doctrine not less dangerous than the counter-doctrine of the divine right of kings. What was more popular in its day than the Crimean war? What has the world thought of it since? Are not many of us old enough to recall how the Treaty of Versailles was acclaimed by multitudes? Who is there today so poor as to do it reverence? To cite an instance nearer home, how many of the enthusiastic supporters of the Congress-Muslim "pact" of 1916 have not lived to regret that mistake ? "A widespread political doctrine" Mr. Bertrand Russell says, "has as a rule two very different kinds of causes. On the one hand, there are intellectual antecedents : men who have advanced theories which have grown, by development or reaction, from previous theories. On the other hand, there are economic and political circumstances which predispose people to accept views that minister to certain moods." In this is to be sought an explanation of the wide appeal which Mr. Gandhi's teachings have made. Mr. Russell says that "no man thinks sanely when his self-esteem has suffered a mortal wound". Mr. Gandhi came out with his slogan of non-cooperation just when the "mortal wound" of Jallianwala Bagh was fresh in India's mind. The same thinker says further : "There are at most times all sorts of doctrines being preached by all sorts of prophets, but those which become popular must make some special appeal to the moods produced by the circumstances of the time." The decay of reason in politics, Mr. Russell says at another place, is a product of two factors, one of which is that "there are classes and types of individuals to whom the world as it is offers no scope". According to him "the fever of nationalism is one form of the cult of unreason" and this, he says, makes strife inevitable.

Seed-beds of revolution

The late Begum of Bhopal told Lord Meston, and he repeated to me the observation, that the seed-beds of revolution are the hunger of the masses and the discontent of the classes. Her Highness, who by common consent was a great stateswoman, warned that Lieutenant-Governor of the United Provinces that both conditions were present in British India. What is the greatest fact about the India of today ? POVERTY. A former Secretary of State, who later became a pillar of the tory party, the Duke of Argyll, said that while he knew poverty in Europe there was not in any other country such "grinding poverty" as was the lot of the people of India ; while it was the considered opinion of the greatest student of Indian economics, Dadabhai Naoroji, that British rule had done the greatest material injury to the people of this country. Mr. John Adam remarked that "India is the richest of countries and Indians are the poorest people". The classes have their self-respect hurt at every turn by the fact of political subjection. "The tallest of us" said Mr. Gokhale before the Welby Commission, "have to bend to suit the exigencies of the present system." We wish to be in our country what other peoples are in theirs, but we are not. On the top of these two permanent factors of the situation come temporary occurrences such as the martial law administration in the Punjab and the excesses of the periodical repression campaigns, which are not calculated to make the people more philosophical in their outlook. Such was the political soil in which Mr. Gandhi planted the seeds, first of non-cooperation and next of civil disobedience. Here was a leader of the highest spiritual eminence, of the most exalted personal character, of rare sacrifice and selflessness, a very Sanyasi who came before a hungry and discontented people and told them that here was the panacea for all their ills. Human nature being as it is, there is little wonder that his message travelled far and wide into town and country and caught on like fire.

Liberal opinion

On the other side is Liberal opinion. Patriotic it is true, wise and appropriate to the circumstances of the country at least as I think, it is not sponsored by an heroic soul like Gandhi. It is so compounded of prosaic fact and uninspiring reason that it can make no wide popular appeal. "Liberalism" as remarked by one British observer, "depends too much on fine perceptions of right and wrong and shuns crude assertion or violent appeals to the emotions." At least if it had been possible for the Liberals to point to the responsiveness of the Government to appeals to its reason things might have been somewhat different, but governments are notoriously not wise. Least of all, alien bureaucracies.

Government's responsibility

When I think of the various occasions on which the Government could have strengthened both itself and the advocates of constitutional methods by timely and reasonable concessions to public opinion and by ameliorative measures which would have mitigated the hard lot of the poor; when I think of how a little sympathy, a little humanness, would have gone far to heal lacerated hearts, and when I think of the persistent thoughtlessness with which the Government has thrown away every such opportunity, and not only by avoidance of right but by positive wrong-doing made a gift to the Congress of thousands of new supporters, I can but exclaim with the old Persian sage "See, my boy, with how little wisdom the world is governed !" While the Government has to thank itself for its utter unpopularity and for the distrust with which it is viewed by the man in the street, the Liberal party has been the principal loser from its irresponsibility aggravated by its unresponsiveness. It is difficult for a constitutional party to thrive under a government that is not constitutional.

Why Liberals cannot join the Congress

In the circumstances it is a pertinent question why the Liberals adhere to their old method instead of swelling the ranks of Congressmen. The answer has been given in part in a previous passage. It may be supplemented very briefly. When they see the condition of the country—the hopeless disunity among the people, the relations of the several communities, the minorities' unwillingness to accept the decisions of the majority, the application by contending parties to sectional and sectarian strife of energy which should have been concentrated on national work for the achievement of Swaraj, our utter incapacity (due to British fault) to assume responsibility for the defence of the country, the continued existence of social customs and institutions which are a negation at once of social efficiency and national unity—Liberals are overwhelmed by the inevitable thought of the immense preparation that must precede the employment of heroic political methods which are certain to bring forth severe retaliation in answer. They cannot, without being intellectually dishonest, without being false to the country, affect belief in the propriety, the wisdom or the efficacy of the methods of the present-day Congress, and if they are not true to themselves they cannot be true to the country. It would be best for the country if there were more of tolerance and judgment in the Congress, more of sacrifice in the Liberal party, more of trust between one community and another, a spirit of accommodation all around. One could wish that the lesson, true for all time, taught by Richard Baxter was read, marked, learnt and inwardly digested by all public men of India, *viz.*, "In things essential Unity, in things non-essential Liberty, in all things Charity".

Constitutional advance

The next point for consideration is whether the survey that has been made of political developments in India leads to the conclusion that there has been constitutional advance. My opinion is that there has been but it is not adequate. As we have seen, the Governor-General's Legislative Council was established in 1854 with no single nonofficial member. The first Indian Councils Act was passed in 1861 and a few nonofficials were nominated by the heads of Government as members. Thirty-one years passed before the next step was taken. Then there was the Indian Councils Act of 1892 which made some advance over conditions then existing. The country had to wait not for thirty-one but only for seventeen years for the next step forward. The Morley-Minto councils brought into being under the Act of 1909 were unsatisfactory enough in all conscience. But who will say that they were not a substantial improvement over the councils which functioned under the Act of 1892 ? For the fourth Act we had to wait for only ten years. The Montagu reforms are popularly voted a failure. I share this opinion to the extent that the results have been far less satisfactory than anticipated. The responsibility for this must be shared with the Government by the Congress. I have uniformly held the opinion that the Montagu Act would not have so disappointed expectation if the National Congress had followed a consistent policy of participation in the work of the councils. Nationalist opinion would then have been so strong that even the bureaucracy of India would not have dared so to disregard it as it in fact has done. True enough it is that governments in India have done nearly all they could to frustrate the purposes of the noble author of the reforms of 1919. But it is not less true that they have only been able to do so, at least in part because of the unreason of the Congress. Sixteen years have elapsed since the Act of 1919 and we have had a new Act this year. I have sufficiently expressed my view of its nature and need not repeat myself. But the point that is here relevant is that the idea of progress has remained alive, and, thanks to the nationalist movement, the British Government have not thought it prudent to make stagnation their policy. Certainly they have done their worst to make the new reforms as useless as possible by taking full advantage of the disordered condition of Indian public life. But I see one element of hope even in this. It lies in the large extension of the franchise. To give the vote to millions of new people, to fill the councils with much larger numbers of members elected by these millions of voters, and then to shackle those councils instead of giving them real power to do what they think to be right, is an act of political unwisdom from the point of view of the present monopolists of power but an act to be welcomed by reformers dissatisfied with the present Act, as the certain result of the new constitution will be an immense growth of discontent and consequently of agitation.

One real and great advance has been the admission of Indians into the inner counsels of the Government. The Congress itself did not think of asking for this until about the year 1904. Its first resolution on executive councils was passed in the year 1897. Read it today and say what you must think of our advance since then. I remember in 1899 a resolution which Mr. R. C. Dutt proposed from the chair in the subjects committee of the Lucknow Congress urging the appointment of Indians to executive councils, was thought to be too radical and had to be withdrawn, not even Mr. Tilak pressing for it. For the first time in 1907 two Indians—Sir K. G. Gupta and Mr. Syed Husain Bilgrami—were appointed to the India Council. Two years later came the first Indian member of the Executive Council of the Governor-General and he was followed by Indian members in Madras, Bombay and Bengal. The House of Lords twice rejected Government proposals to establish such a council in the United Provinces. But see now. There are three Indians in the Executive Council of the Governor-General, two in Madras and Bengal, and one each in other provinces. And there is no province, however small, which has no such council. Then there are so many ministers, all of them Indians. The advance made in this direction would have been incredible in the pre-Montagu years. Look again at Indians in the Privy Council, including its Judicial Committee. And at the present numbers of Indian High Court judges. When first Lord Ripon appointed an Indian (Sir Romesh Chunder Mitter) as an acting Chief Justice, the British in India could not easily reconcile themselves to the innovation. Since then many Indian judges has acted as chief justices, while two have held the position substantively. One Indian was a member of the House of Lords, parliamentary under-secretary and the Governor of a province. Several Indians have officiated as governors.

The disappointing feature

Acknowledgment of the successive steps in constitutional advance that have been made leads to the enquiry whether they have been accompanied by the transference of real power to the representatives of the people. The answer has to be in the negative. Every time the showy trappings and the costly paraphernalia of government by councils have been made a mask, as it were, to conceal the ugly fact that effective power is retained in the hands of the British. Mr. J. A. Spender, one of the most thoughtful of British publicists, has pointed out that "where the executive functions independently of the legislature and can persist in spite of its displeasure, politicians cannot obtain the power and influence that they enjoy in countries where parliaments are sovereign". He has further told us that "in all constitutions there is an incessant veiled struggle" between the executive and the legislature "for the possession of power". Our legislature has been denied power to make its will prevail.

British Parliament and Indian Legislature

The British House of Commons is a sovereign parliament. This is the principal inducement for the highest talent in the country to seek a place in that house. It is why in the House of Commons speech is "directed to the prac-

22

tical end of governing the country". Blackstone thus defined the position of a member of the House of Commons :

> The Commons consist of the representatives of the nation at large, exclusive of the peerage. Every member, though chosen by a particular district, once he is elected and returned, serves for the whole realm ; the end of his coming thither being not particular but general ; not merely to advantage his constituents but the Commonwealth as a whole.

But how are our councils recruited ? Through more than a dozen of separate and special electorates of communities and interests. This is worse than the British House of Commons would have been if it had consisted of members who were the separate representatives of "the General Medical Council, the Incorporated Society of Lawyers, the Institute of Journalists, the Authors' Society, the various federations and associations of employers with which the country abounds" (J. A. Spender : *The Public Life*). Our councils do include representatives of landlords' associations, chambers of commerce and such like bodies ; but they also include representatives separately elected on a communal register of Muslims, Europeans, Anglo-Indians, Indian Christians, Sikhs, depressed classes, women, etc. Because of the power of Parliament in England "the parliamentary career is the public life and a man cannot hope to rise to eminence unless he is a good parliamentarian". "In America" however, "membership of Congress leads nowhere in itself, and may even be a disqualification unless a man has power and capacity which makes him formidable outside Congress". But then in America democratic government functions through an elected head of the executive, the President. Our councils are more like the old Reichstag, of which it was said that it supplied "a false facade of democracy to a system which was essentially autocratic and bureaucratic". It was said of the Reichstag that it was "composed of three dozen skilful and clever men and 350 idiots who are indifferent to the progress of business". I shall not be surprised if our bureaucracy's estimate of our M.L.A.'s and M.L.C.'s is somewhat like this and they may be of opinion that it would be quite wrong to invest such bodies with anything like real power. They may further think that notwithstanding the coming extension of the franchise the legislatures of India will still be so insufficiently representative of the people at large that to transfer power to them will be to place it in the hands of an Indian oligarchy. One answer to this may well be that in India an Indian oligarchy is any day better than a non-Indian bureaucracy. But there is another answer. What was the state of the House of Commons before the successive reforms of 1832, 1867, 1884 and 1918 made it what it is today? What was its representative character? Here is an authoritative description of the position as it was :

> In this old regime the average politician counted for little except when the spoils were distributed. The great majority attached themselves to their patrons—the Bedfords, the Butes and the Rockinghams, and were content to vote dutifully and take their pay, or when not voting dutifully to exact their price. The last thing their patrons expected or desired of them was that they should meddle in politics outside the course laid down for them in parliament. Three-fourths of the House of Commons represented either close boroughs which were the acknowledged property of territorial magnates or rotten boroughs which were for sale or purchase and when knocked down to the highest bidder, were absolutely in his gift. The so-called representative system was three centuries out of date, and even if it had not been vitiated by the efforts of the Tudor sovereigns to establish a Court party by a profuse creation of boroughs most of which fell into the hands of neighbouring landowners, would have been reduced to absurdity by the natural shifts and changes of policy. Oldfield reports that as late as 1815 the House of Commons contained 471 members who owed their seats to the goodwill and pleasure of 144 peers and 123 commoners, 16 government nominees, and only 171 members elected on popular suffrages. The latter came mainly from county constituencies and great towns which were strong enough or public-spirited enough to resist the sale of their privileges, but the cost of contesting this was so great that their representation fell almost inevitably into the hands of the great and the wealthy. Out of a population of eight millions of the English people only 165,000 possessed a vote. (J.A. Spender, *The Public Life*, vol. 1, pages 6 & 7.)

Formation of Cabinets in England

And how about the formation of the governments responsible to Parliament ? British political biographies teem with instances of appointments the most unsuitable made for reasons unrelated to the public interest. Here are a few instances :

Disraeli, forming an Administration, offered the Board of Trade to a man who wanted instead the Local Government Board, as he was better acquainted with the municipal affairs of the country than its commerce. 'It does not matter,' said Disraeli ; 'I suppose you know as much about trade as Blank, the First Lord of the Admiralty, knows about ships.'

Richard Lalor Sheil, asked why he was appointed President of the Board of Trade, said, 'I think the only reason is I was found to know less of trade than any other man in the House of Commons.'

John Bright, appointed President of the Board of Trade: 'so unfitted was he for administration, he did not know even how to tie up official papers with red tape'.

Palmerston, having fixed upon Sir George Cornewall Lewis for the office of Secretary of State for War, argued the point with Lady Theresa Lewis, saying that the duties would not be military, but civil. 'He would have to look after the accounts,' said the Prime Minister. 'He never can make up his own,' said the wife. 'He will look after the commissariat,' said the Prime Minister. 'He cannot order his own dinner,' replied the wife. 'He will control the clothing department,' said the Prime Minister. 'If my daughters did not give the orders to his tailor, he would be without a coat,' replied the wife.' Cornewall Lewis, however, accepted the offer.

Once there was a difficulty in finding a Colonial Secretary, Lord Palmerston said, 'Well, I'll take the colonies myself,' and presently remarked to the Clerk of the Privy Council; 'Just come upstairs with me for half an hour and show me where these places are on the map.'

Charles James Fox is said to have confessed his ignorance of what Consols meant. He gathered from the newspapers that they were 'things which rose and fell'; and he was always delighted when they fell, because he noticed, that for some unaccountable reason, it very much annoyed Pitt, as Chancellor of the Exchequer.

The son and biographer of Lord Randolph Churchill has told that when, as Chancellor of the Exchequer, Treasury returns worked out in decimal figures were laid before him, he inquired what 'these damned dots' signified.

Sir Edward Carson, speaking as First Lord of the Admiralty in 1917, during the Great War, declared that he entered the Admiralty in a state of extreme ignorance.

"Some one asked me the day I went there how I felt, and I said, 'My only qualification is that I am absolutely at sea'[1].

Dickens made the following ironic commentary on the formation of a Government :—

> The limited choice of the Crown in the formation of a new Ministry would be between Lord Coodle and Sir Thomas Doodle, supposing it to be impossible for the Duke of Foodle to act with Goodle, which may be assumed to be the case, in consequence of the breach arising out of that affair with Hoodle. Then, giving the Home Department to Joodle, the Exchequer to Koodle, the Colonies to Loodle, and the Foreign Office to Moodle, what are you to do with Noodle ? You can't offer the Presidency of the Council. That is reserved for Poodle. You can't put him in the Woods and Forests. That is hardly good enough for Quoodle. What follows ? That the country is shipwrecked, lost, and gone to pieces because you can't provide for Noodle !

Yet did it occur to anybody to deprive the House of Commons of its powers of a sovereign parliament because its character was such as this and the governments responsible to it were formed in this manner ? Not only is it that our councils can never avoid the paralysing consciousness that what they say may not prevail,—and actually does not on the most important occasions,—there is another source of demoralization. It can be indicated in the following sentence of Mr. Spender's : "In some countries the distribution of decorations has even been raised to a fine art as a means of checking independent opinions or methods of behaviour which the Government may think inconvenient." All things considered, the debates in our councils, though sometimes they rise to a high level, are as "though conducted in an atmosphere which has been compared to that of a ducal mansion with the duke lying dead upstairs".

Restraint of press

Measures restrictive of the liberty of the press, to which reference has been made, have the effect of curtailing political freedom, of the people as a whole. Along with security

1. *The Pageant of Parliament* by Michael MacDonagh, vol. 1, p. 143.

of person and property, the freedom of speech and of association, the liberty of the press, the right of public meeting, and freedom of conscience are among the fundamental rights of civilized mankind which a civilized government must be slow to interfere with and ought not to restrict save under the stress of grave emergency and then only for the duration of the emergent state and to no greater extent than absolutely necessary. If these principles were disregarded in the Sedition Act of 1898, they were simply cast to the winds in the Press Act of 1910, the Princes' Protection Acts of 1922 and 1934, the Press Ordinances of 1930 and 1932, and the Criminal Law Amendment and Special Powers Acts of 1931, 1932 and 1935. Special measures investing the executive with wide powers of control over the press, which were first put forward as temporary and intended for an emergent situation, have this year been made permanent by the central Government and extended for five years by several provincial governments. Doubtless as a preparation for and in harmony with the large reforms which are expected to be brought into effect about a year hence in the provinces! I suppose our future "autonomous governments responsible to elected legislatures" have to be protected in this very progressive manner even in their pre-natal stage by the bureaucracy which will dry-nurse them. For the bureaucracy is likely still to be in the seat of power, whoever may be in office as ministers. Leaving on one side the cynicism which moved a great newspaper proprietor to say that "the power of the press is the suppress", I would cite the following observations of an honoured and veteran publicist on the position of the press and of Government's manipulation of it :—

"In a modern community the newspaper is an essential part of government by the people." "The press might get on without politics, but politics cannot get on without the press." "Government themselves have been among the worst offenders in the manipulation of the press; and to increase their control would be the means of extinguishing their critics and making the rest their tools."

The double fact of the situation with regard to the press is that while the people have by dint of sacrifice and persistence built up a press in India, the state has, by successive decrees ratified by a weak legislature, curtailed its freedom and virtually made the Government its master.

Reality and appearance

What I have said proves that the criticism is well-founded that amid all the show of a concession which the British Government and Parliament make they take good care not to part with the substance of power. But Indian opinion has so learnt to discount appearances and to insist upon the substance and conditions in India have so deteriorated economically and so changed politically that the first and last test of an act which purports to be a measure of reform is now and will be henceforward, does any reality underlie it ?

In the administrative sphere

In the administrative sphere there has been some progress in some directions. The greatest of administrative reforms is the Indianization of the superior services. In the army the only change for the better has been the negative one of the removal of the race barrier and the affirmative one of exceedingly slow progress in the appointment of Indians as King's commissioned officers. In the Indian Civil Service an examination is now held in India without prejudice to the Indian candidates sitting at the London examination. But a step backwards has now been taken by power being given to the Secretary of State to determine how many of the Indians who pass the London examination he will or will not admit into the service regardless of the place they obtain. Undeserved concessions were made to officers of all-India services by the unwanted Lee Commission of 1923, of course at the expense of the Indian taxpayer, and they will continue to be enjoyed by the favoured recipients. On the whole there has been progress with Indianization. But it is less than it may well have been and than the country both deserves and requires. The great and urgent reform of the separation of judicial and executive functions still remains a hope of the future. It must necessarily happen that in the administrative system, which is regulated by executive order, sometimes something good, sometimes something bad is done. On the whole I think the conclusion would not be justified either that there has nowhere been a change for the better or that such improvement has been effected as to satisfy even moderate reformers.

There has been real progress in local self-government. Our district and municipal boards are today more of self-governing bodies than a generation ago.—Tenant rights have received greater recognition, but the position is still far from satisfactory and there is urgent need of more progressive agrarian legislation. But it should not be such as to be even capable of being described as expropriatory. For example, landlords should nowhere be treated as Inamdars have been in the recent amendment of the Madras Estates Land Act. The legislation I contemplate will, while securing landlords in their just rights, make unfairness to tenants a legal impossibility.—The most gratifying progress has been the increase in the number of regional universities and the recognition of the teaching university as a better type than the affiliating variety. I am speaking under the auspices of one of the new universities, and both as an Indian and as an Andhra—a native of this very district.—I cordially wish it every prosperity. Andhra University has the proud distinction of having as its vice-chancellor the most learned, most brilliant and most famous son of Andhradesa now living. Sir Radhakrishnan has acquired by sheer merit an international reputation and made of himself a national asset.—Research has made remarkable progress during recent years and there are today in India scholars and scientists of whose contributions to knowledge their countrymen have reason to be proud.

Having spoken of the governments of Indian states, on the whole uncomplimentarily, I must not omit to make honourable mention of some of them, where real progress has been made. Several of the states are well administered; in some there has been constitutional advance. No one can say that Mysore, Travancore and Cochin; Gwalior, Indore and Bhopal; Baroda and Bikaner, Gondol and Bhavnagar are not efficiently administered. It will be a day of pride for Indians when states in general are as well governed as Mysore, for example, and all of them recognise the people's fundamental rights of citizenship.

Hope for the future

If the survey and the observations that have been made should produce a depressing thought in a single mind my purpose has been ill-served. The conclusion that I draw from the events of the last three quarters of a century is that the work that has been done should fill us with hope for the future. The lesson that it conveys is that the sons and daughters of India should bend every particle of their energy to the unselfish service of the Motherland in the faith that India never can die, and howsoever bitter may be the disappointments of today her future is bound to be glorious. No one who looks beneath the surface of things will either be unduly sanguine of the near future or be weighed down by pessimism about the ultimate end of our national effort. Remember that the orator of the Congress spoke not only of "the brilliant achievements of the past" and "the dismal failures of the present" but of "the splendid possibilities of the future".

"The real, the ultimate secret of democracy is the leadership of moral virtue," says Lord Lothian. "For" he adds, "unless democracy can throw up enough people who would take moral principle as their guide at whatever cost democracy releases passions and animosities which destroy it, and drive people back to some kind of absolutism as the one means of tranquillity and peace."

How does the moral principle operate in public life ? Says Lord Lothian :

It is not very easy to describe how moral principle operates in public life. It is unselfish fidelity to what one believes to be right, not surrender to political animosity, in any form. It is fearless readiness to face facts as they are, and to deal with them as they are, and not fanatical disregard of everything which seems to run counter to one's own preconceived ideas. It is an unselfish readiness to forego personal ambition or profit, place or power, for the sake of the common good. It is determination to do what one believes the public good really requires and not merely what is popular or what the crowd demands. It is readiness to face abuse and unpopularity, not from one's opponents, for that is easily sustained, but from those whom you seek to help and on whose support you rely. It is wisdom, unselfishness, self-control in the face of temptation and pressure to short cuts and easy ways.

The widest diffusion of education, the development of public spirit by increasing numbers of the educated, statesmanship among leaders and discipline in the rank and file, sacrifice wisely directed, constant effort to draw the communities nearer to one another in mutual trust, the eradication as far as possible of differential treatment based upon distinctions of birth and sex, above all, a living faith in the beneficent purposes of Providence—these are certain to lead India onward and upward until she becomes the land of free men, happy and prosperous, honoured by the nations, and, most important of all, moral and spiritual as becomes the land of the Vedas and Vedanta. God bless India. I conclude with the prayer—

ओं सहना ववतु सहनौ भुनक्तु,
सह वीर्यं करवाव है ।
तेजस्विनावधीतमस्तु, माविद्विषाव है ॥

INDEX